THE SURVIVE AND THRIVE GUIDE

An Illustrated Book with Tips, Techniques, and Quotes on Dealing with the Challenges in Your Life

by Gini Graham Scott, Ph.D.

THE SURVIVE AND THRIVE GUIDE

Copyright © 2020 by Gini Graham Scott

All rights reserved. No part of this book may be used or reproduced by any means, graphic, electronic, or mechanical, including photocopying, recording, taping or by any information storage retrieval system without the written permission of the author except in the case of brief quotations embodied in critical articles and reviews.

TABLE OF CONTENTS

INTRODUCTION 7
PART I: DEALING WITH YOUR FEELINGS OF ANGER 9
AN INTRODUCTION TO PART I 10
THE PERVASIVENESS OF ANGER 11
THE DESTRUCTIVENESS OF ANGER 15
    The Consequences of Anger 17
    Harming Yourself 20
    Making Mistakes, Regrets, and Repentance 23
    The Danger of Seeking Revenge 27
    Anger and Loss 30
    The Danger of Anger to Society 33
ANGER AND TRUTH 35
CONTROLING ANGER 39
MAKING CHOICES 49
LETTING GO OF ANGER 57
EXPRESSING YOUR ANGER 67
THE IMPORTANCE OF FORGIVENESS 71
ANGER, UNDERSTANDING AND EMPATHY 75
PROMOTING CHANGE 79
ANGER, FEAR, AND SADNESS 87
ANGER AND DENIAL 91
ANGER AND REASON 95
ANGER AND OTHERS 103
ANGER, LOVE AND BETRAYAL 109
WHEN ANGER BECOMES FUN 113
WHAT TO DO WHEN YOU OR SOMEONE ELSE IS ANGRY 117
    Dealing with Your Anger in Resolving a Conflict 118
    Other Ways to Deal with Your Anger 120
ANGER QUESTIONNAIRE 125

PART II: DEALING WITH YOUR FEAR AND ANXIETY	129
INTRODUCTION TO PART II	130
THE DANGER OF FEAR	131
CONQUERING AND OVERCOMING FEAR	137
HAVING COURAGE	147
DO IT ANYWAY	161
UNDERSTANDING FEAR AND CHANGING YOUR MINDSET	173
TECHNIQUES FOR OVERCOMING YOUR FEARS	179
PART III: TAPPING INTO YOUR COURAGE	189
INTRODUCTION TO PART III	190
OVERCOMING FEAR	191
FACING FAILURE	201
TAKING ON CHALLENGES AND RISKS	205
ACCOMPLISHING GOALS AND ACHIEVING SUCCESS	215
HAVING FAITH	221
FREEDOM, INDEPENDENCE, AND CREATIVITY	225
OTHER QUALITIES OF COURAGE	229
APPLYING THE PRINCIPLE OF COURAGE IN YOUR LIFE	237
PART IV: FINDING FORGIVENESS FOR OTHERS AND YOURSELF	243
INTRODUCTION TO PART IV	244
FORGIVENESS AND THE DIVINE	245
FORGIVENESS AND LOVE	249
FORGIVENESS AND COMPASSION	253
FORGIVENESS AND PEACE	257
FORGIVENESS, STRENGTH, AND COURAGE	261
FORGIVENESS AND LETTING GO, MOVING ON, AND NEW BEGINNINGS	265
FORGIVENESS, MAKING MISTAKES, AND ACCEPTANCE	271
FORGIVENESS AND FORGETTING	275
THE IMPORTANCE OF FORGIVING OTHERS	279
FORGIVING ENEMIES	283
THE DIFFICULTY OF FORGIVENESS	287

FORGIVENESS AND PERMISSION 291
APPLYING THE PRINCIPLE OF FORGIVENESS IN YOUR LIFE 295
PART V: FEELING GRATITUDE 301
INTRODUCTION TO PART V 302
THE VALUE OF GRATITUDE 305
EXPRESSING GRATITUDE 311
GRATITUDE ABOUT YOURSELF 317
HAPPINESS 321
RELATIONSHIPS 331
APPRECIATION 343
SAYING THANKS 355
ACHIEVEMENT 365
CONTENTMENT AND ACCEPTANCE 371
LEARNING AND EXPERIENCE 377
FAITH 381
ABUNDANCE 393
FUTURE BENEFITS 399
GIVING 405
HAVING A POSITIVE ATTITUDE 409
APPRECIATING LIFE 415
ANIMAL EMOTIONS 427
PEOPLE WHO ARE NOT GRATEFUL 431
HUMILITY 437
APPLYING THE GRATITUDE OUTLOOK IN YOUR LIFE 441
ABOUT THE AUTHOR 447

INTRODUCTION

Life has become even more challenging for everyone due to the pandemic, the collapsing economy, and most recently protests about racial injustice. But life has always involved overcoming a series of challenges -- from mastering new assignments and experiencing conflicts at work to dealing with issues in personal relationships. Indeed, from the beginning of human history -- and prehistory, individuals have always faced different kinds of obstacles to overcome, and the stories shared over campfires and in books, theatrical performances, and films are all about overcoming challenges -- and the stock market goes up and down depending on how well companies meet current challenges or are expected to meet challenges in the future.

I thought about how meeting such challenges go back to the beginning of time upon seeing a recent *Netflix* reality show *Alone: The Arctic.* in which 10 contestants who already have wilderness skills are each placed in a separate location near a large lake. They have a limited number of tools, such as an ax, knife, and twine, and have to build their own shelters and find food through hunting and gathering, much like the early humans did. Adding to the challenge, they are in an extremely hostile, dangerous environment, where they face even more intense difficulties to survive -- with a goal of being the last survivor to win a half a million dollars.

The Survive and Thrive Guide is designed to help you successfully overcome any type of challenges you face. The focus is on dealing with the emotional reactions that occur, which can be organized into five stages of response. These are:

- experiencing feelings of anger about what has happened,
- feeling fear and anxiety about the effects of this challenge and your ability to confront it,
- tapping into your feelings of courage to help you get through any obstacles that are standing in your way,
- expressing forgiveness to others who contributed to this challenge and to yourself for any mistakes you made along the way,
- feeling gratitude because of what you achieved or did to overcome the challenge, and what you learned no matter the results of your efforts.

To this end, this book is divided into five parts that were originally published as separate books on each emotion: *The Anger Book; How to Understand and Deal with Your Fear and Anxiety, The Courage Book, The Forgiveness Book,* and *The Gratitude Book.*

Each part begins with an introduction, followed by a series of sections, with an introduction to the quotes in that section and photos illustrating the quotes. Each section ends with tips on how you can apply these ideas in your life.

As you read the book takes notes on how you can apply these ideas, and if any quotes resonate with you, try putting them on cards or posters, so you can refer to them to inspire and motivate you.

PART I: DEALING WITH YOUR FEELINGS OF ANGER

AN INTRODUCTION TO PART I

Commonly, you can feel anger in confronting a challenge, because you may feel frustrated and irritated by having to face the situation. You may feel anger at the person or persons who are part of this situation or have led you into having to deal with what occurred. You may see them as obstacles, rivals, or otherwise in the way of what you want to do. Or you may experience anger for other reasons.

Whatever the source of your anger, it can have negative consequences, such as a loss of friendship, love, and support. It can even escalate a conflict into a life and death struggle. But at other times, anger can fuel creative and positive change in oneself, in one's relationships, and in society as a whole. So a good strategy is to control and manage that anger by acting from choice and wisdom to do the right thing. For anger is one of the mechanisms that contribute to one's survival and success when it is used effectively.

The following chapters feature the comments and quotes of many well-known persons about dealing with anger, along with illustrations that reflect these sentiments. The quotes are organized by the different themes reflected in these comments, which include:
- the pervasiveness of anger,
- the consequences of expressing anger,
- understanding the reasons for anger,
- how anger can hurt you,
- how anger can alienate you from others,
- how to control or get rid of your anger.

I have included the source for each comment, although sometimes these attributions draw on an even earlier source, such as ancient Greek writers and Buddhist sages. Where it's known, I have included the original source.

THE PERVASIVENESS OF ANGER

Anger is everywhere, since it is a survival mechanism that helps us be assertive in threatening situations or at times when we need to overcome a challenge to gain an advantage. It helps us fight if necessary. Sometimes, anger can be a response to a perceived problem -- from anger at oneself for an error or flaw to anger against other individuals or society as a whole.

But at other times, anger can lead to great suffering, as well as the angry person being negatively viewed by others. Often a person who is angry will find still more reason to be angry, because of these feelings of suffering or being rejected by others. And commonly responding with anger can become a habit, so those angry feelings are even more likely to grow.

In short, anger is pervasive. Sometimes it can be used for the good, but often it leads to negative consequences.

The following quotes describe how this anger can turn into a common response to everything or gain disapproval from others.

"Show me an angry man, and I'll show you someone who gets things done."
Anonymous

"Anger is like food for the soul. It helps one survive and thrive, since anger teaches us to fight when necessary, just as flight can help us get away when it makes no sense to fight."
Anonymous

"He that will be angry for anything will be angry for nothing."
Sallust, Roman historian and politician, 86-35 BC

"Everybody in America is angry about something."
Anthony Braxton, American composer and instrumentalist

"One effect of an individualistic culture that's poor at instilling mutual respect is that people jump more quickly to anger or violence."
Geoff Mulgan, CEO of the National Endowment for Science, Technology, and the Arts (NESTA)

"I am awfully greedy; I want everything from life…It is difficult to get all which I want. And then when I do not succeed I get mad with anger."
 Simone de Beauvoir, French novelist, political activist, and social theorists. Author of *The Second Sex*. 1908-1986.

THE DESTRUCTIVENESS OF ANGER

Often anger is viewed as a destructive force, whereby if you feel and express your anger, this will come back to harm you. In effect, your anger will backfire on you. As much as you might feel a satisfied releasing your anger by attacking someone to get revenge or justice, in the end, that expression will be punished. You will poison your psyche, as if you have drunk or eaten some toxic substance. It's like the law of attraction or karma coming back to even the score. So you have to face the consequences of your anger, because if you say or do something in the heat of anger, you may regret it later.

Another reason to avoid erupting in anger is that this belittles you. It makes you seem a lesser person to others, because you can't control your anger. In fact, from a spiritual perspective, becoming angry diminishes you and your soul, whereas showing warmth, kindness, and friendliness, all opposites of anger, makes you become bigger, like a brighter star in the sky.

Additionally, anger can harm others, as well as yourself.

Thus, the message here is not to give in to your uncontrollable anger. Find a way to channel or manage it constructively. Otherwise your anger will come back to bite you, like an angry dog or cat you kick on the street.

The following quotes express this theme.

The Consequences of Anger

"Anger is a brief madness."
Horace, Roman poet, 65-8 BC.

"Anger does not solve anything; it builds nothing."
Thomas S. Monson, American religious leader, author, and president of the Church of Jesus Christ of Latter-Day Saints

"You will not be punished for your anger; you will be punished by your anger."
Guatama Buddha, Indian sage, 564/480-483/400 BC

"Anger is as a stone cast into a wasp's nest."
Pope Paul VI, Bishop of Rome, leader of the worldwide Catholic Church from 1963-1978.

"Expressing anger is a form of public littering."
Dr. Willard Gaylin, Clinical Professor of Psychiatry at Columbi College of Physicians and Surgeons.

"Don't you know the sound of anger brings a dark result. And every insult is like a lightning bolt."
Third Eye Blind, American 90's rock band

"When anger rises, think of the consequences."
Confucius, Chinese teacher, philosopher, 551-479 BC

"How much more grievous are the consequences of anger than the causes of it."
Marcus Aurelius, Roman Emperor from 161-180 AD, author of *Meditations*

"Whatever is begun in anger ends in shame."
Benjamin Franklin, American statesman, editor, inventor 1706-1790

Harming Yourself

"Every time you get angry, you poison your own system."
Alfred A. Montapert, philosopher, 1907-1997.
Author of *The Supreme Philosophy of Man*

"Anger is an acid that can do more harm to the vessel in which it is stored than to anything on which it is poured."
Mark Twain, American writer, humorist, 1835-1910
Author of *The Adventures of Tom Sawyer*

"Holding anger is a poison. It eats you from inside. We think that hating is a weapon that attacks the person who harmed us. But hatred is a curved blade. And the harm we do, we do to ourselves."
Mitch Albom, American author, screenwriter, broadcaster, musician
Author of *The Five People You Meet in Heaven*

"At some point it doesn't matter who was right and who was wrong. At some point, being angry is just another bad habit, like smoking, and you keep poisoning yourself without thinking about it."
Jonathan Tropper, American writer and professor
Author of *This Is Where I Leave You*

"The anger welled inside me, with nowhere to go. I could feel it eating away at me. I knew if I didn't find a way to release it, it would destroy me."
Kami Garcia, American writer of children's fantasy and sci-fi
Author of *Sublime Creatures*

"I am a danger to myself if I get angry."
Oriana Fallaci, journalist, author, political interviewer, 1929-2005

Making Mistakes, Regrets, and Repentance

"Anger is the most impotent of passions. It effects nothing. It goes about, and hurts the one who is possessed by it more than the one against whom it is directed."
Carol Sandburg, American poet, writer, and editor, 1878-1967

"Anger is stupid, and stupidity will kill you more surely than your opponent's blade."
Patricia Briggs, American writer of fantasy
Author of *Dragon Bones*

"Angry people are not always wise."
Jane Austen, English novelist, 1775-1817
Author of *Pride and Prejudice*

"Anger is useful only to a certain point. After that, it becomes rage, and rage will make you careless."
Lauren Oliver, American author of young adult books
Author of *Pandemonium*

"Getting angry doesn't solve anything."
Grace Kelly, American actress, princess of Monaco, 1929-1982

"Anger is a killing thing: it kills the man who angers, for each rage leaves him less than he had before – it takes something from him."
Louis L'Amour, American novelist of western, historical fiction, and sci-fi, 1908-1988
Author of *The Walking Drum, The Haunted Mesa*

"Never do anything when you are in a temper, for you will do everything wrong."
Baltasar Gracian, Spanish philosopher, 1601-1658
Author *The Art of Worldly Wisdom*

"Keep your temper. A decision made in anger is never sound."
Ford Frick, American sports writer and baseball executive, 1894-1978

"The one who cannot restrain their anger will wish undone what their temper and irritation prompted them to do."
Horace, Roman poet, 65-8 BC

"Speak when you are angry – and you'll make the best speech you'll ever regret."
Groucho Marx, American comedian, film and TV star, 1870-1977

"An angry man is again angry with himself when he returns to reason."
Publilius Syrus, Latin writer, 85-41 BC
Known for his moral sayings, called "sententiae"

"Anger begins with folly, and ends with repentance."
Beverly Sills, American opera singer, 1929-2007

The Danger of Seeking Revenge

"A man that studieth revenge keeps his own wounds green."
Francis Bacon, English philosopher, 1561-1626
Advocate for the scientific method

"While seeking revenge, dig two graves – one for yourself."
Douglas Horton, American Protestant clergyman, 1891-1968

"When everything that you know and love…is taken from you harshly…all you can think about is anger, hatred, and even revenge…and no one can save you."
Masashi Kishimoto, Japanese manga artist
Created the "Naruto" manga series

"If you spend your time hoping someone will suffer the consequences for what they did to your heart, then you're allowing them to hurt you a second time in your mind."
Shannon L. Alder, inspirational author
Wrote the most inspirational quotes on "Goodreads"
Author of *300 Questions to Ask Your Parents Before It's Too Late*

"There is nothing worse than having an enemy who is a total loser. It's incredibly frustrating when seeking revenge against one, because you come to the realization that there is really nothing you can do to make the person's life worse than it already is. They have nothing to take; there is no way to screw them over if you have been their victim. It's maddening."
Ashly Lorenzana, sex worker, freelance wirter
Author of *Sex, Drugs, and Being an Escort*

"You cannot get ahead while you are getting even."
Dick Armey, American politician. Former U.S. Represemtative from Texas and House Majority Leader

"When a man points a finger at someone else, he should remember that four of his fingers are pointing at himself."
Louis Nizer, American lawyer, 1902-1994
Author of *My Life in Court*

Anger and Loss

"There is a natural law of karma that vindictive people, who go out of their way to hurt others, will end up broke and alone."
Sylvester Stallone, American actor
Best known as writer and actor in *Rocky*

"Anger makes dull men witty, but it keeps them poor."
Francis Bacon, English philosopher, 1561-1626
Advocate for the scientific method

"Anger is an expensive luxury in which only men of certain income can indulge."
George William Curtis, American writer and public speaker for African-American equality and civil rights, 1824-1892

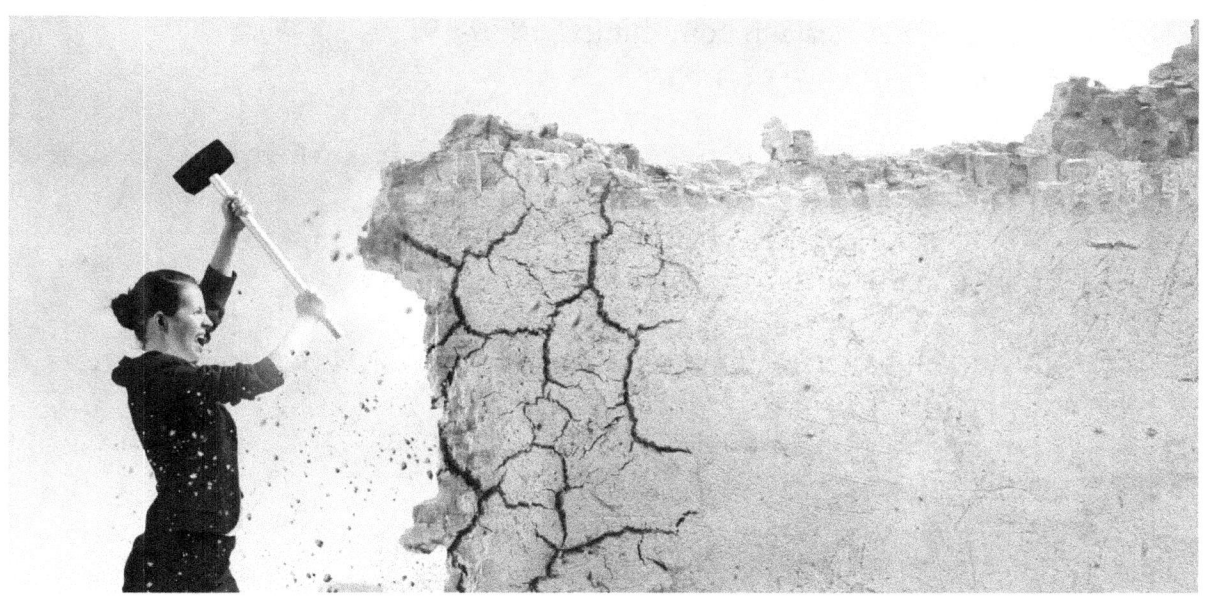

"If a small thing has the power to make you angry, does that not indicate something about your size?"
Sydney J. Harris, American journalist, 1917-1986
Columnist of "Strictly Personal"

"Anger, resentment and jealousy doesn't change the heart of others – it only changes yours."
Shannon L. Alder, inspirational author
Wrote the most inspirational quotes on "Goodreads"
300 Questions to Ask Your Parents Before It's Too Late

"I shall allow no man to belittle my soul by making me hate him."
Booker T. Washington, American educator, writer, leader of the African-American community, 1856-1915
Author of *Up from Slavery*

"Indulge not thyself in the passion of anger; it is whetting a sword to wound thine own breast, or murder thy friend."
Akhenaton, Egyptian pharaoh of 18th dynasty, 1353-36 BC
Founded new cult dedicated to Aton, the sun disk

"A broken bone can heal, but the wound a word opens can fester forever."
Jessamyn West, American author, 1902-1984
Author *The Friendly Persuasion*

The Danger of Anger to Society

"Anger is the enemy of non-violence and the price is a monster that swallows it up."
Mahatma Gandhi, Indian independence movement leader, 1869-1948
Inspired movement for civil rights and freedom across the world

"Extremism thrives amid ignorance and anger, intimidation and cowardice."
Hillary Clinton, American politician and nominee for President in 2016 election campaign

ANGER AND TRUTH

At times, anger can be a negative emotion that can rage out of control and become very destructive and harm both others and oneself, like a fire expanding in a conflagration. But one of the positives of anger is that it is associated with honesty and truth. Though one needs to control its expression and seek its release to feel better, the source of that anger can be recognizing the truth.

This truth of anger comes about because it expresses what one is truly feeling, regardless of whether the information it is based on is true or false. That's because the honesty of anger springs from within, from understanding the way things are. It does not depend on the honesty of what is without.

As a result, a person can be very much deluded based on misinformation and flights of fantasy. But the anger itself accurately reflects what one is feeling about something; it taps into one's current understandings of how things are, or it provides an immediate emotional response to a situation that is occurring or has just occurred.

For example, while road rage can be very destructive, it expresses an emotional truth, though it is best to deflect, avoid, or tamp down that anger.

The following quotes deal with this theme of truth.

"Anger cannot be dishonest."
Marcus Aurelius, Roman Emperor, from 162-280 AD

"The truth will set you free, but first it will piss you off."
Joe Klaas, author and news reporter, 1920-2016
Author of *Twelve Steps to Happiness*

"Anger at lies lasts forever. Anger at truth can't last."
Greg Evans, American cartoonist
Creator of comic strip "Luann"

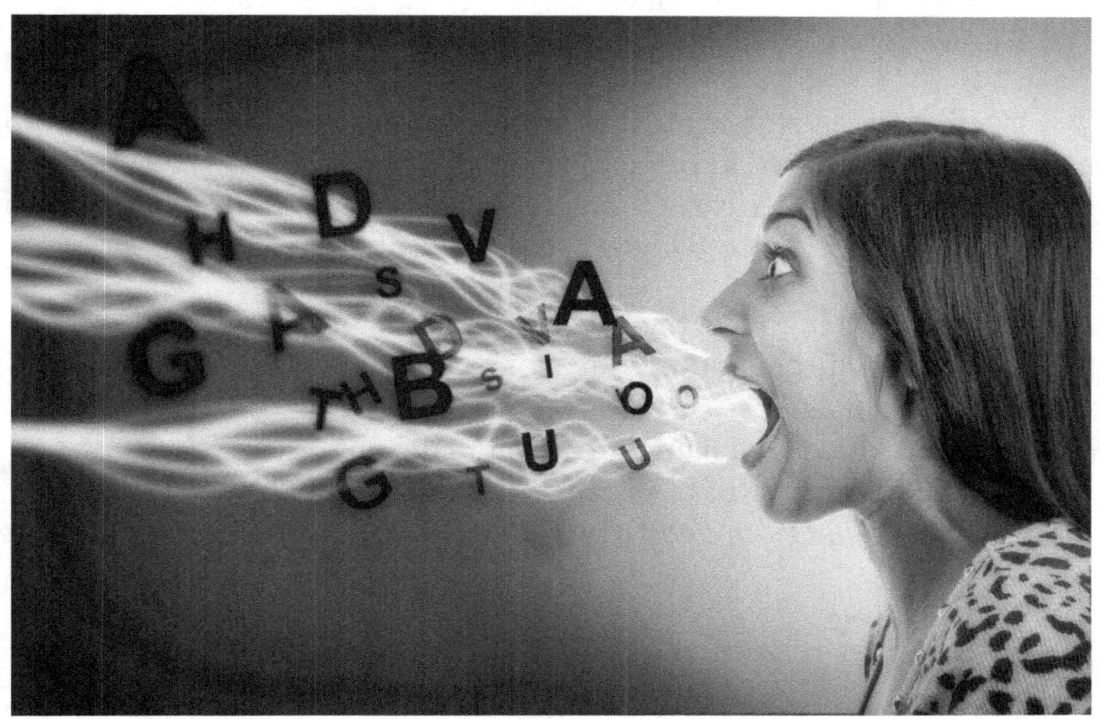

"Words can be said in bitterness and anger, and often there seems to be an element of truth in the nastiness. And words don't go away, they just echo around."
Jane Goodall, British anthropologist, known for her work with gorillas

"Never forget what a man says to you when he is angry."
   Henry Ward Beecher, American clergyman, 1813-1887
   Known for his support of abolition of slavery

"Defeat anger, stop using it as a shield against truth, and you will find the compassion you need to forgive the people you love."
   Glenn Beck, American TV and radio host, conservative commentator
   Author of *The Seven Wonders that Will Change Your Life*

"It is important to feel the anger without judging it, without attempting to find meaning in it. It may take many forms: anger at the health-care system, at life, at your loved one for leaving. Life is unfair. Death is unfair. Anger is a natural reaction to the unfairness of loss."
   Elizabeth Kubler-Ross, American psychiatrist, 1926-2004
   Author of *On Death and Dying*

CONTROLING ANGER

No matter how angry you feel, you can learn to control that anger. You can variously channel it, direct it, release it in harmless and productive ways, or let it go, rather than expressing it in a verbal or physical explosion of emotion. As part of this control, you can choose what you want to do with the energy of that anger and how you want to direct it. Also, you can find a more effective way to let the anger go that won't backfire on you.

Initially, though, take charge of your anger, so you don't angrily say things you will later regret. You don't want to physically attack someone which could escalate the situation and result in physical harm to you or the other person. It could even lead to a criminal case that could have lasting repercussions long after the anger that fueled the explosion of rage is gone.

Still another reason for controlling your anger is that just being angry doesn't fix the problem. Moreover, if you let others make you angry, you have given up your power of control to them.

Instead, when you feel angry, you want to direct that anger against an appropriate target, so you can release it in an appropriate way You don't want to take out your anger on the wrong target, such as when a person who is angry at a parent or boss takes it out on someone who is weaker and more vulnerable. Or if you are feeling generally out of sorts and angry at the world or at yourself, find a way to target and channel that anger safely and sanely, so the anger doesn't grow within you, only to explode later or at an inappropriate target.

The following quotes reflect this theme.

"Anger is a momentary madness, so control your passion or it will control you."
G. M. Trevelyan, British historian 1876-1962
Author *England in the Age of Wycliffe*

"Venting doesn't soothe anger; it fuels it."
Susan Cain, American writer and lecturer
Author of *Quiet: The Power of Introverts in a World That Can't Stop Talking*

"The best fighter is never angry."
Lao Tzu, Chinese philosopher and writer, 6th-5th century to 531 BC

"Anger, if not restrained, is frequently more hurtful to us than the injury that provokes it."
Lucius Annaeus Seneca, Roman stoic philosopher, 4 BC-65 AD

"The greatest remedy for anger is delay."

Thomas Paine, American political activist, philosopher, 1737-1809
Founding Father of the U.S.

"When angry count to ten before you speak. If very angry, count to one hundred."
Thomas Jefferson, American statesman, 1743-1826

"When angry, count to four; when very angry, swear."
Mark Twain, American writer, humorist 1835-1910
Author of *The Adventures of Tom Sawyer*

"The best remedy for a short temper is a long walk."
Joseph Joubert , French moralist/essayist, 1754-1824
Known for *Pensees*

"Always write angry letters to your enemies. Never mail them."
Josh Silver, founder and CEO of Represent US, challenging big money in politics
"When you are angry try your best to go to sleep. It keeps you away from speaking, writing and thinking while you are angry."

Amit Kalantri, Indian writer
Author of *I Love You, Too* and *One Bucket of Tears*

"Be modest, humble, simple. Control your anger."
Abraham Cahan, Jewish-American socialist, newspaper editor, novelist, and politician, 1860-1951

"The finest fury is the most controlled."
Christopher Hitchens, Anglo-American journalist and social critic
Author of *Love, Poverty, and War: Journeys and Essays*

"The anger of a person who is strong, can always bide its time."
James Whitcomb Riley, American writer and poet, 1849-1916

"Do not follow vain desires; for verily he who prospers is preserved from lust, greed and anger."
Abu Kakr, adviser to the prophet Muhammed, 573-634 AD

"Mixing defensiveness with anger – a wonderful mix."

Liza Palmer, American writer
Author of *Seeing Me Naked* and *Conversations with the Fat Girl*

"Conquer the angry one by not getting angry; conquer the wicked by goodness; conquer the stingy by generosity, and the liar by speaking the truth."
Guatama Buddha, Indian sage, 564/480-483/400 BC

"Speak the truth, do not become angered, and give when asked, even be it a little. By these three conditions one goes to the presence of the gods."
Gautama Buddha, Indian sage, 564/480-483/400 BC

"Anger is a valid emotion. It's only bad when it takes control and makes you do things you don't want to do."
Ellen Hopkins, young adult novelist and poet
Author of *Fallout*

"Anger…it's a paralyzing emotion…you can't get anything done…It's helpless…It's absence of control…And I need all my skills, all of the control, all of my powers…and anger doesn't provide any of that – I have no use for it whatsoever."
Toni Morrison, American novelist and editor
Radio interview September 15, 1987.

"Anger is like flowing water; there is nothing wrong with it as long as you let it flow. Hate is like stagnant water; anger that you denied yourself the freedom to feel, the freedom to flow; water that you gathered in one place and left to forget…Allow yourself to feel anger, allow your waters to flow, along with all the paper boats of forgiveness."
C. JoyBell C., feminist thinker and writer
Frequently quoted author on "Goodreads"

"I would not look upon anger as something foreign to me that I have to fight…I have to deal with my anger with care, with love, with tenderness, with nonviolence."
Thich Nhat Hanh, Vietnamese Buddhist monk and peace activist
Author of *Being Peace*

"There are two types of seeds in the mind: those that create anger, fear, frustration, jealousy, hatred, and those that create love, compassion, equanimity ad joy. Spirituality is germination and sprouting of the second group and transforming the first group."
Amit Ray, Indian author and spiritual master

"I know of no more disagreeable situation than to be left feeling generally angry without anybody in particular to be angry at."
Frank Moore Colby, American educator and writer, 1865-1925

"He who angers you conquers you."
Elizabeth Kenny, Australian nurse, known for new approach for treating poliomyelitis, 1880-1952

"I came to realize that if people could make me angry they could control me. Why should I give someone else such power over my life?"
Ben Carson, American retired neurosurgeon
Author of *Gifted Hands: The Ben Carson Story*

"Speak the truth, do not become angered and give when asked, even be it a little. By these conditions one goes to the presence of the gods."
Gautama Buddha, Indian sage, 564/480-483/400 BC

"It is okay of talking about the past, as long as there's no bitterness and anger. It only gives you a heart attack. It won't change the past either."
Ann Marie Aguilar, Associate Director of Wellbeing and Sustainability at Arup Associates

"Very often in everyday life one sees that by losing one's temper with someone who has already lost his, one does not gain anything but only sets out upon the path of stupidity. He who has enough self-control to stand firm at the moment when the other person is in a temper, wins in the end."
Hazrat Inayat Khan, founder of the Sufi Order, 1882-1927
Author of *Mastery through Accomplishment*

"Often we allow ourselves to be upset by small things we should despise and forget. We lose many irreplaceable hours brooding over grievances that, in a year's time, will be forgotten by us and by everybody. No, let us devote our life to worthwhile action and feelings, to great thoughts, real affections, and enduring undertakings."
Andre Maurois, French author, 1885-1967

"Declare your jihad on thirteen enemies you cannot see – egotism, arrogance, conceit, selfishness, greed, lust, intolerence, anger, lying, cheating, gossiping and slandering. If you can master and destroy them, then you will be ready to fight the enemy you can see."
Al-Ghazali, Muslim theologian, philosopher, mystic, 1058-1111

MAKING CHOICES

Often getting angry is associated with a loss of control, when an outraged person gives vent to that anger. Perhaps one can exercise control in choosing the target, but otherwise, letting go can mean smashing things, sending nasty letters, seeking revenge, or other means of expressing outrage.

However, you don't have to express that anger. You can exercise control by choosing to express that feeling or not. Likewise, you can choose ways to let go, such as forgiving whoever made you angry, throwing yourself into another activity so your angry feelings go away, or directing your anger into improving yourself, your workplace, or your community. Thus, in these various ways, you can choose to not feel angry about something; or you can channel that anger so you are in charge in how you express it, when, in what form, and to whom.

The following quotes describe how you can choose what to do with whatever makes you angry.

"Every day we have plenty of opportunities to get angry, stressed or offended. But what you're doing when you indulge these negative emotions is giving something outside yourself power over your happiness. You can choose not to let little things upset you."
Joel Osteen, American Televangelist
Author of *Your Best Life Now* and *Become a Better You*

"It is impossible for you to be angry and laugh at the same time. Anger and laughter are mutually exclusive and you have the power to choose either."
Dr. Wayne Dyer, American doctor and speaker on self-development
Author of *Your Erroneous Zones*

"The madder it makes you, the harder you need to laugh at it."
Destiny Booze, romance, suspense, and thriller author

"Love is better than anger. Hope is better than fear. Optimism is better than despair. So let us be loving, hopeful and optimistic. And we'll change the world."
Jack Layton, Canadian politician and opposition leader, 1950-2011

"Patience is the direct antithesis of anger."
Allan Lokos, Founder and teacher, the Community Meditation Center
Author of *The Pocket Peace: Effective Practices for Enlightened Living*

"Anger begs more anger, and forgiveness and love lead to more forgiveness and love."
Mahavira, Founder of Jainism, 599-527 BC

"Anybody can become angry – that is easy, but to be angry with the right person and to the right degree and at the right time and for the right purpose and in the right way – that is not within everybody's power and is not easy."
Aristotle, Greek philosopher, 384-322 BC

"Anger is just anger. It isn't good. It isn't bad. It just is. What you do with it is what matters. It's like anything else. You can use it to build or to destroy. You just have to make the choice."
Jim Butcher, American writer of fantasy book series
Author of *White Night*

"There are two things a person should never be angry at, what they can help, and what they cannot."
Plato, Greek philosopher, 428-348 BC

"To rule one's anger is well; to prevent it is better."
Tryon Edwards, American theologian, 1809-1894
Compiled *A Dictionary of Thoughts*

"Anger – a better alternative to caffeine."
Ilona Andrews, American writer of fantasy and romantic fiction
Author of *Magic Rises*

"In certain situations, manifesting anger is the right attitude; in others it is not the right thing to manifest because it will only add to violence. In the first case, anger unblocks the conflict and causes another to become more conscious. In the latter, it only adds to the unconsciousness and inflames the conflict."
Jean-Yves Leloup, French writer, philosopher, and theologian
Author of *Compassion and Meditation: The Spiritual Dynamic Between Buddhism and Christianity.*

"Kindness is strength. Good-nature is often mistaken for virtue, and good health sometimes passes for genius. Anger blows out the lamp of the mind. In the examination of a great and important question, everyone should be serene, slow-pulsed, and calm. Intelligence is not the foundation of arrogance. Insolence is not logic. Epithets are the arguments of malice."
Robert G. Ingersoll, American lawyer, political leader 1833-1899
Author of *The Christian Religion An Enquiry*

"If you stay in the company of anger, pain, or hurt, happiness will find someone else to visit. Make the choice to view all of your past relationships as a gift. Throw out what hasn't worked in the past and incorporate new concepts. Focus on being happy."
Kristen Crockett, Speaker, facilitator, and life coach
Author of *The Gift of Past Relationships*

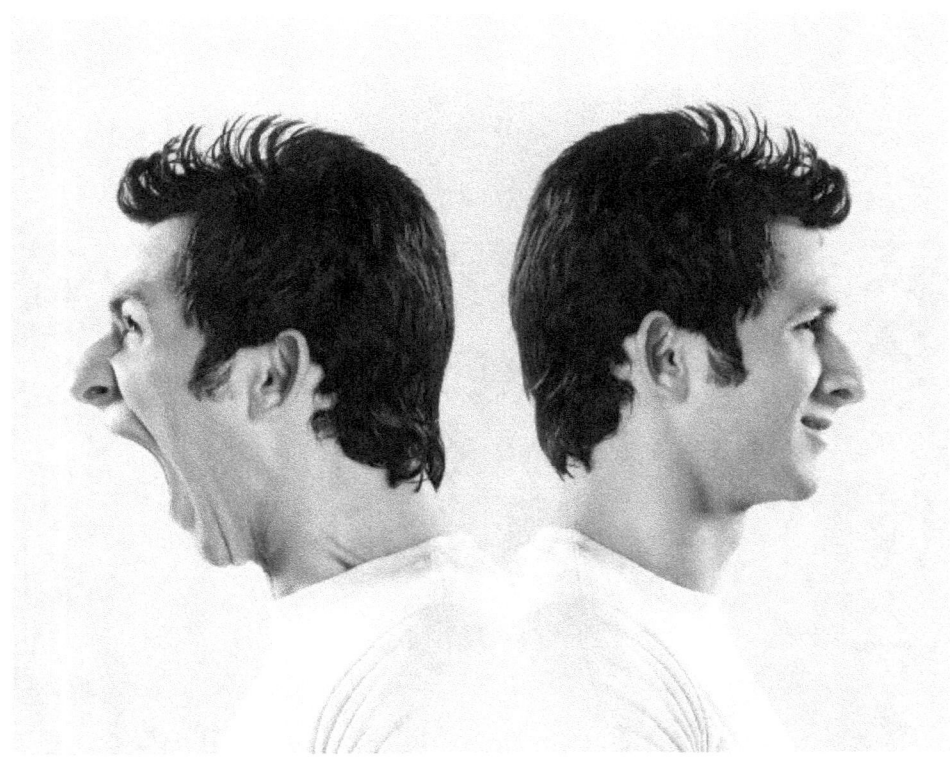

"If you are driven by fear, anger or pride nature will force you to compete. If you are guided by courage, awareness, tranquility and peace, nature will serve you."
    Amit Ray, Indian writer and spiritual master
    Author of *Nonviolence: The Transforming Power*

"To be angry is to yield to the influence of Satan. No one can make us angry. It is our choice. If we desire to have a proper spirit with us at all times, we must choose to refrain from becoming angry. I testify that such is possible."
    Thomas S. Monson, American religious leader, author, and president of the Church of Jesus Christ of Latter-Day Saints

"He best keeps from anger who remembers that God is always looking upon him."
    B. C. Forbes, Scottish-born American financial journalist, 1880-1854
    Founder of *Forbes Magazine*

LETTING GO OF ANGER

Once you get angry, another key to dealing with it is to learn to release it and let it go, however you choose to do so. You don't have to express your anger outwardly, but you need to release it somehow, so the anger dissipates. Otherwise, it can grow and fester within you, like a bad seed or fungus that takes root and within you and spreads.

Physically, the anger that remains within can take various forms, such as developing an ulcer or high blood pressure. Emotionally, you might feel stressed, anxious, or sad. Mentally, you might find yourself distracted and have difficulty concentrating. You may not remember as well or think as effectively as before. It is as if the anger is taking away from your usual physical, emotional, and mental resources like a sponge, sucking up your energy and vitality. Or perhaps think of your anger like a sinkhole, pulling you down, or a ball of burning wood, searing your insides. There are various analogies, but the essence is that holding in your anger is like having a toxic waste, virus, or disease ravaging your body, emotions, mind, and spirit or soul.

How do you let this anger go? There are different strategies, from engaging in other activities to looking at a calming image, such as a flower or beautiful landscape.

The following quotes express this theme.

"Get mad, then get over it."
Colin Powell, American states and retired 4-Star U.S. Army general

"Holding on to anger is like grasping a hot coal with the intent of throwing it at someone else; you are the one who gets burned."
Gautama Buddha, Indian sage, 564/480-483/400 BC

"Holding onto anger is like drinking poison and expecting the other person to die."
Gautama Buddha, Indian sage, 564/480-483/400 BC

"Holding a grudge and harboring anger/resentment is poison to the soul. Get even with people…but not those who have hurt us, forget them, instead get even with those who have helped us."
Steve Maraboli, speaker, author, and behavior scientist
Author of *Unapologetically You*

"Let today be the day you finally release yourself from the imprisonment of past grudges and anger. Simplify your life. Let go of the poisonous past and live the abundantly beautiful present…today."
Steve Maraboli, speaker, author, and behavior scientist
Author of *Unapologetically You*

"At times anger will trigger harsh words. After a cooling period wisdom sets in; finally, the ability to speak from the heart with love and compassion."
Ana Monnar, educator
Author of *Relax: New and Selected Poems*

"Letting go gives us freedom, and freedom is the only condition for happiness. If, in our heart, we still cling to anything – anger, anxiety, or possessions – we cannot be free."
Thich Nhat Hanh, Vietnamese Buddhist Monk and peace activist
Author of *The Heart of the Buddha's Teaching: Transforming Suffering Into Peace, Joy, and Liberation*

"For every minute you remain angry, you give up sixty seconds of peace of mind."
Ralph Waldo Emerson, American writer, transcendentalist 1803-1882
Author *Nature*

"Don't hold to anger, hurt or pain. They steal your energy and keep you from love."
Leo Buscaglia, aka "Dr. Love," American author, speaker, 1924-1998

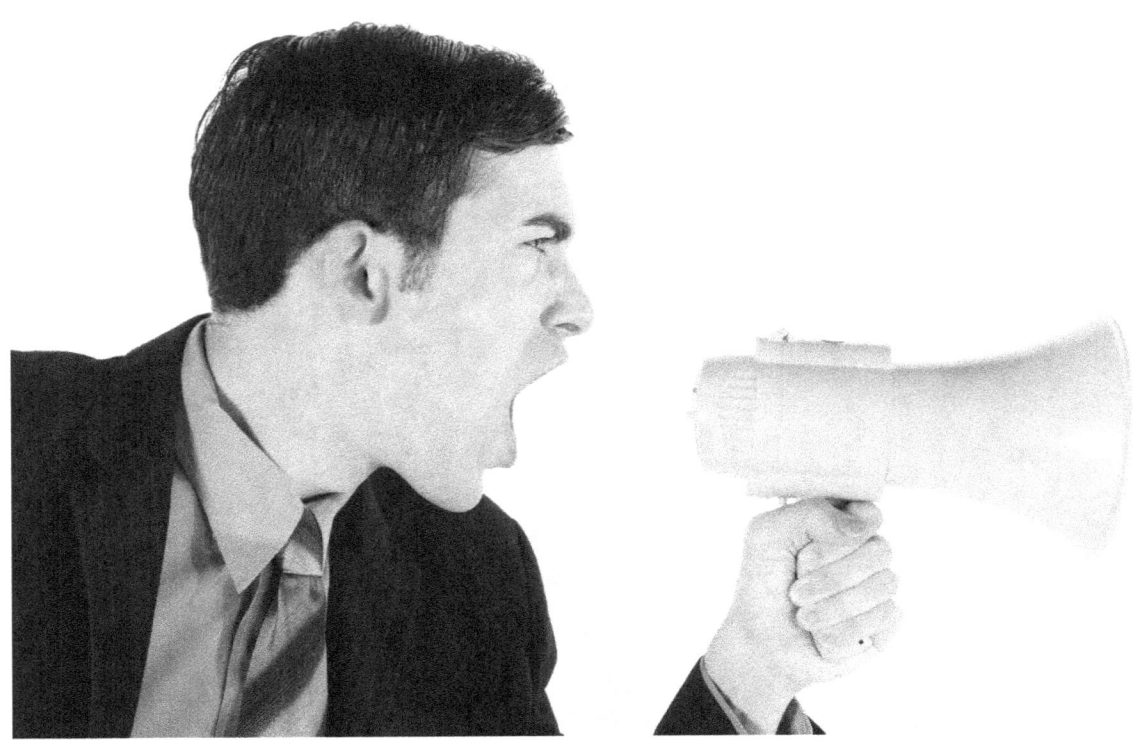

"Life's not that simple. Not so easy to move on when the anger you've got is what keeps you going."
Rachel Ward, English-born Austrian actress, director, screenwriter
Author of *Numbers*

"It is…important to avoid terrible arguments or expressions of outrage. You should steer clear of emotionally damaging behavior. People forgive, but it is best not to stir things up to the point at which forgiveness is required."
Andrew Solomon, writer and lecturer on psychology, politics, the arts
Author of *The Noonday Demon: An Atlas of Depression*

"I realized that if my thoughts immediately affect my body, I should be careful about what I think. Now if I get angry, I ask myself why I feel that way. If I can find the source of my anger, I can turn that negative energy into something positive."
 Yoko Ono, Japanese multimedia artist, singer, songwriter
 Widow of singer-songwriter John Lennon

"I'd be lying if I said I wasn't angry some days. But I really have worked hard to put a lot of the anger and disappointment in the past."
Monica Lewinsky, American TV personality, fashion designer
Known for being a White House intern under President Bill Clinton

"Never go to bed angry. Stay up and fight."
William Congreve, English playwright and poet, 1670-1729

"Make sure you never, never argue at night. You just lose a good night's sleep, and you can't settle anything until morning anyway."
Rose Kennedy, American philanthropist and socialite, 1890-1995

"Man should forget his anger before he lies down to sleep."
Thomas de Quincey, English essayist, 1785-1859
Author of *Confessions of an English Opium-Eater*

"Anger ventilated often hurries towards forgiveness; anger concealed often hardens into revenge."
    Edward G. Bulwer-Lytton, English novelist, playwright, 1803-1873

"It doesn't pay to say too much when you are mad enough to choke, for the word that stings the deepest is the word that is never spoke."
    Jules Renard, French wrtier, 1864-1910
    Author of *Poil deCarotte*

"I was angry with my friend:
I told my wrath, my wrath did end.
I was angry with my foe:
I told it not, my wrath did grow."
William Blake, English poet, painter, printmaker, 1857-1827

"Nobody can keep on being angry if she looks into a heart of a pansy for a little while."
L. M. Montgomery, Canadian writer
Author of novel series, *Anne of Green Gables*

# EXPRESSING YOUR ANGER

While there are all kinds of admonitions to control your anger, find other alternatives, or let your anger go, sometimes you can experience a positive release by expressing and venting that anger. Though do so in a way that doesn't create more problems, such as by escalating anger into rage, saying words you later regret, or destroying a once valued relationship.

Sometimes expressing anger can counter more destructive emotions, such as feeling sad, depressed or hopeless. And sometimes just saying words you have long held back can help to clear the air, rather than leaving you feelings regret because you said nothing.

The key is to find a balance, when you express that anger as a part of the letting go process. In effect, letting off steam can release the pressure, much like taking off a cover to let off steam when boiling water in a teakettle. Otherwise the steam will build up so much that the kettle can explode. Likewise, you need to let your anger out, so you can feel comfortable and calm again.

The following quotes reflect the need to express this anger.

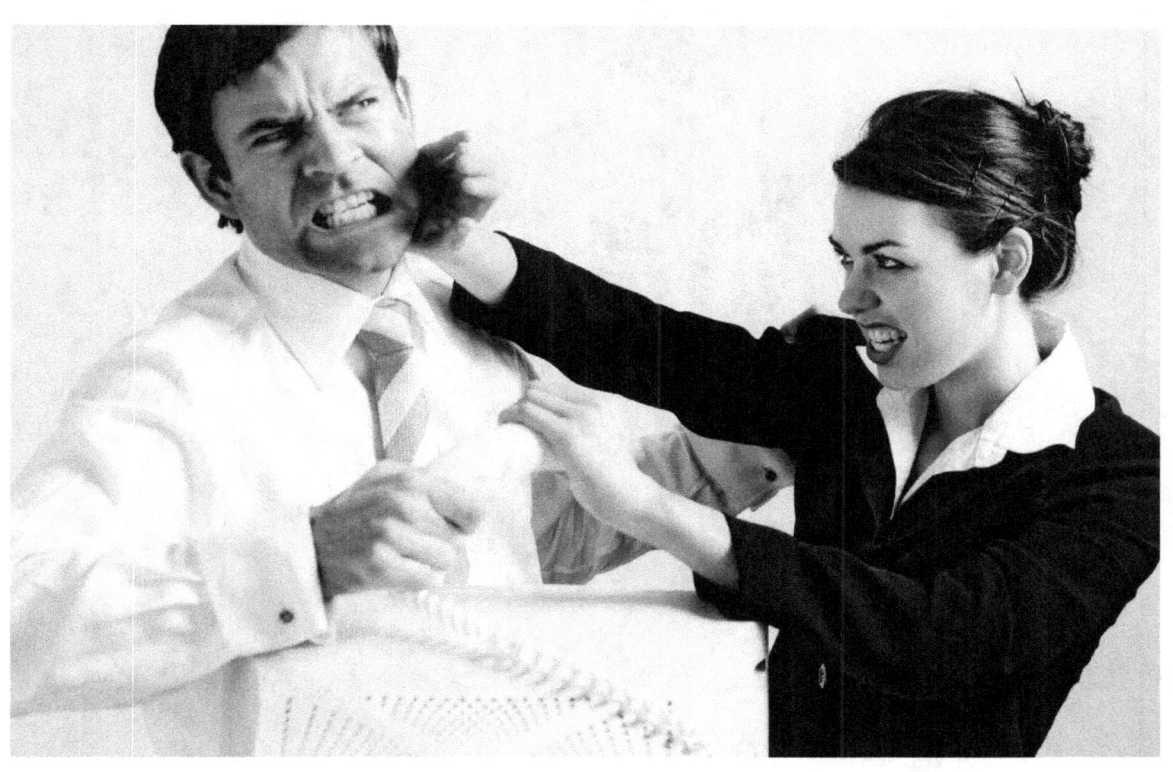

"Red-hot anger takes away a lot of the heartache."
    Victoria Ashton, American writer
    Author of *Juicy Secrets, Confessions of a Teen Nanny* and *Rich Girls*.

"Anger as soon as fed is dead.
Tis starving makes it fat."
Emily Dickinson, American poet, 1830-1886
Author of *Selected Poems*

THE IMPORTANCE OF FORGIVENESS

A key part of letting go of anger is forgiveness. You experience a release from the tension caused by anger when you forgive the person who caused your anger by what they said or did. Otherwise, that anger can fester and grow like a deadly fungus, or it can remain ready to go off once triggered like a grenade that lies in wait.

But if you forgive, you destroy the fungus by shining a light of healing on it. Or you pull the trigger out of the grenade before it can go off, so the grenade becomes inert. Likewise, forgiveness makes it possible to let go and move on. While time might eventually provide that healing, forgiving now speeds up the process. You forgive, and once you forgive, you let go.

The following quotes reflect this power of forgiveness.

"When you hold on to anger and unforgiveness, you can't move forward."
Mary J. Blige, American singer, songwriter, producer, actress

"Forgiveness is the economy of the heart…forgiveness saves the expense of anger, the cost of hatred, the waste of spirits."
Hannah More, English religious writer, philanthropist, 1745-1833

"Life is so short. The only person you hurt when you stay angry or hold grudges is you. Forgive everyone, including yourself."
Tom Giaquinto, writer
Author of *Be a Good Human*

"Anger makes you smaller, while forgiveness forces you to grow beyond what you are."
Cherie Carter-Scott, writer, life coach, and motivational speaker
Author of *If Life Is a Game, These Are the Rules*

"Anger is an essential part of being human. People are taught to deny themselves anger, and in this, they are actually opening themselves up to hate. The more you deny yourself the freedom to be angry, the more you will hate. Let yourself be angry, and hate will disintegrate, and when hate disintegrates, forgiveness prevails!"
C. JoyBell C., feminist thinker and writer
Frequently quoted author on "Goodreads"

ANGER, UNDERSTANDING AND EMPATHY

Sometimes anger at others comes from misunderstanding and miscommunication. You do not recognize what others are thinking or feeling when they act, so you interpret their intentions in a negative light. For example, you interpret something as a sign of disrespect or betrayal, when the other person didn't intend it that way. In response, you can get angry for no good reason, and this conflict can escalate, like a seed that grows into a plant, watered by anger born of a communications mix-up and misunderstood meanings.

By contrast, when you understand or empathize with someone else, this can help to avoid or end a conflict. This can lead to friendship and mutual support, rather than the anger that turns one person, group, or community against another.

Then, too, should you become angry at someone for a fault they have rather than trying to understand that person, this anger might lead you to help that person if you can or recognize your own flaws in order to let go and correct them.

The following quotes express this importance of understanding and empathy to overcome anger.

"The opposite of anger is not calmness, it's empathy."
Mehmet Oz, aka "Dr. Oz," American doctor, author, and TV personality

"You reclaim your power by loving what you were once taught to hate."
Bryant H. McGill, author, activist, and social entrepreneur

"I don't like anybody to be angry with me. I'd rather have friends."
B. B. King, American blues singer, songwriter, record producer

"When you are offended at any man's fault, turn to yourself and study your own failings. Then you will forget your anger."
Epictetus, Greek philosopher, 55-135 AD

PROMOTING CHANGE

While anger is commonly viewed as a negative emotion to be avoided or controlled, it has a positive side, if it can be channeled into something constructive. As such, it can result in making changes in oneself, such as redirecting one's anger towards oneself for doing something wrong or turning a failure to achieve a goal into behaving differently to attain that goal or find success in another way.

Anger can also mobilize people to work together because of something they are angry about, resulting in changes in the neighborhood, in local government policies, or in something that makes people angry. So anger becomes a vehicle for social or political change. Moreover, if enough people share this anger, they can bring about change in their county, region, state, or country. Fueled by anger, changes of all sorts are possible.

Likewise, anger in the workplace or about social issues can result in changes in companies, in educational systems, or in any kind of organization. In turn, this kind of anger can act as a kind of cleansing, burning away what is bad in order to provide a place for new growth.

The following quotes show how anger can become a vehicle for change of all sorts.

"There is nothing wrong with anger provided you use it constructively."
Wayne Dyer, American doctor and speaker on self-development
Author of *Your Erroneous Zones*

"It is wise to direct your anger towards problems – not people; to focus your energies on answers – not excuses."
William Arthur Ward, American motivational speaker, 1921-1994
Author of *Fountains of Faith*

"Anger can be a problem, but it has tremendous potential, too. It's just figuring out what to do with it."
Sean Penn, American actor, filmmaker, and political activist

"Experiencing sadness and anger can make you feel more creative, and by being creative, you can get beyond your pain or negativity."
Yoko Ono, Japanese multimedia artist, singer, songwriter
Widow of singer-songwriter John Lennon

"In times of great stress or adversity, it's always best to keep busy, to plow your anger and your energy into something positive."
Lee Iacocca, American auto executive, known for developing Ford Mustang and Pinto, author of *Iacocca: An Autobiography*

"Good satire comes from anger. It comes from a sense of injustice, that there are wrongs in the world that need to be fixed. And what better place to get that well of venom and outrage boiling than a newsroom, because you're on the front lines."
Carl Hiassen, American journalist and novelist

"Usually when people are sad, they don't do anything. They just cry over their condition. But when they get angry, they bring about change."
James Russell Lowell, American romantic poet, 1819-1891
Author of *A Fable for Critics*

"Sometimes, you have to get angry to get things done."
Ang Lee, American film director, screenwriter, and producer
Director of *Life of Pi* and *Crouching Tiger, Hidden Dragon*

"Everybody…perceives me as being angry. It's not anger, it's motivation."
Roger Clemens, retired American baseball pitcher

"Bitterness is like cancer. It eats upon the host. But anger is like fire. It burns it all clean."
Maya Angelou, American poet/civil rights activist, 1928-2014
Author of *I Know Why the Caged Bird Sings*

"The world needs anger. The world often continues to allow evil because it isn't angry enough."
Bede Jarrett , English Dominican friar, 1881-1934
Author of *Medieval Socialism* and *The Emperor Charles IV*

"Usually when people are sad, they don't do anything. They just cry over their condition. But when they get angry, they bring about change."
Malcolm X, Muslim minister and human rights activist, 1925-1965

"There was never a social change in American without angry people

at the heart."
Keith Miller, Australian test cricketer and air force pilot, 1919-2004

"Anger is wonderful. It keeps you going. I'm angry about bankers. About the government."
Terry Pratchett, English writer of fantasy novels, 1948-2015

"Anger is the prelude to courage."
Eric Hoffer, American social writer and philosopher, 1898-1983

"The best response to terror is righteous anger, confidence in ultimate justice, a refusal to be intimidated."
Dean Koontz, American writer of suspense thrillers
Author of *Velocity*

"Guilt is not a response to anger; it is a response to one's own actions or lack of action. If it leads to change then it can be useful, since it is then no longer guilt but the beginning of knowledge. "
Audre Lorde, African-American civil rights activist, 1934-1992
Author of *Sister Outsider: Essays and Speeches*

"It is hope – with regard to our careers, our love lives, our children, our politicians, and our planet – that is primarily to blame for angering and embittering us. The incompatibility between the grandeur of our aspirations and the mean reality of our condition generates the violent disappointments which rack our days and etch themselves in lines of acrimony across our faces."
Alain de Bottom, *Religion for Atheists*

"When I am angry, I can pray well and preach well."
Martin Luther King, Baptist minister, civil rights leader, 1929-1968

"Constructive anger…also known as passion…Passion has overthrown tyrants and free prisoners and slaves. Passion has brought justice where there was savagery. Passion has created freedom where there was nothing but fear. Passion has helped souls rise from the ashes of their horrible lives and build something better, stronger, more beautiful."
Jim Butcher, American writer of fantasy book series
Author of *White Night*

"Poetry = Anger x Imagination."
Sherman Alexie, American poet, writer, and filmmaker
Author of *One Stick Song*

ANGER, FEAR, AND SADNESS

Often anger is viewed as a response to fear or as a more productive emotion than just being fearful. Similarly it is viewed as better to feel angry than sad. The advantage over feeling fear is that anger can be tamed, released, or directed outward to produce positive change. But fear can lead to anxiety and retreat; it stymies action, unless one acts to overcome that fear. And the sadness that accompanies fear can lead one to feel helpless and lack the energy to do anything.

While fear can be a protective survival mechanism that leads to a beneficial retreat in the face of danger, fear converted into anger can be directed outward into positive action. Likewise, sadness tends to stymie action as it is directed inward into self-criticism and regret. But sadness turned into anger can similarly lead to action with favorable results.

The following quotes reflect this association between fear, sadness, and anger.

"Anger prepares us to fight and fear prepares us to flee."
Chip Heath, American writer and speaker
Author of *Made to Stick: Why Some Ideas Survive and Others Die*

"Fear leads to anger. Anger leads to hate. Hate leads to the dark side."
Bree Despain, American writer
Author of *The Dark Divine*

"Most hatred is based on fear, one way or another. Yeah. I wrapped myself in anger, with a dash of hate, and at the bottom of it all was an icy center of pure terror."
Laurell K. Hamilton, American fantasy and romance writer
Author of *Guilty Pleasures*

"Fear is the only true enemy, born of ignorance and the parent of anger and hate."
Edward Albert, American film and TV actor, 1951-2006

"At the heart of all anger, all grudges, and all resentment, you'll always find a fear that hopes to stay anonymous."
Donald L. Hicks, American writer and poet
Author of *Look into the Stillness*

"Let us not look back in anger, nor forward in fear, but around in awareness."
James Thurber, American cartoonist, writer, 1894-1961
Known for his cartoons and short stories in the *New Yorker*

"Grab the broom of anger and drive off the beast of fear."
Zora Neale Hurston, African-American novelist and anthropologist, 1891-1960

ANGER AND DENIAL

Sometimes anger can be a form of denial, when we don't want to know the truth – or don't want to accept it, because we don't like what the truth tells us about ourselves or others. So we get angry, and this anger becomes like a shield to keep us from the truth.

As such, anger can lead us to ward off information and opinions which counter what we already think and believe, so we continue to hold onto and fight for what is wrong. We are angered by anything or anyone who contradicts what we think what we know to be true. We don't want to acknowledge we have made a mistake, so anger becomes like a shield to protect us from the truth. Anger can also keep us from listening to understand what the other person is saying.

Instead, it is important to look beneath the anger to what has provoked it. At times, of course, we are angry upon learning the truth about something and seek to correct it by striving for change in ourselves, in our relationships, or in our society. But at other times, we get angry to cover-up something – whether to shield ourselves or prevent others from knowing the truth.

An example of how this denial works is when someone questions us about something we don't want them to know. So we react with angry denials. We say: "No, that cannot be" or "No, that wasn't me. But the angry outbursts are designed to cover up what is really real, and others can see through this. They recognize the "bullshit" in what we are saying, so they see that we are trying to cover up something or hold something back. As a result, such a denial born of anger doesn't always work and can produce a backfire effect that hurts us even more.

People can also try to deny their anger to evade their problems and avoid upsetting others. But this denial can leave someone feeling anxious, due to not acknowledging the real anger they feel and finding a more positive, productive way to let that anger go.

The following quotes reflect this use of anger to cover-up the truth.

"In a controversy the instant we feel anger we have already ceased striving for the truth, and have begun striving for ourselves."
Gautama Buddha, Indian sage, 564/480-483/400 BC

"When a man is wrong and won't admit it, he always gets angry."
Thomas Chandler Haliburton, Nova Scotia politician 1796-1865

"There was never an angry man that thought his anger unjust."
Saint Francis de Sales, Swiss clergyman, 1567-1622

"People who are prone to anxiety are nearly always people-pleasers who fear conflict and negative feelings like anger. When you feel upset, you sweep your problems under the rug, because you don't want to upset anyone. You do this so quickly and automatically that you're not even aware you're doing it."
    David D. Burns, professor of psychiatry and behavioral sciences
    Author of *The Feeling Good Handbook*

"How often it is that the angry man rages denial of what inner self is telling him."
    Frank Herbert, American science fiction writer, 1920-1986
    Author of *Dune*

ANGER AND REASON

Sometimes anger is compared with reason and viewed as an irrational or emotional response that can lead to faulty thinking. Or one can become angry due to faulty reasoning. In effect, being angry contrasts with the ideal of being a reasonable, rational person, who thinks and acts reasonably. Viewed in this way, anger can cloud our understanding or prevent us from knowing the truth.

Then, too, without reason, irrational anger can turn into hatred, which can be even more harmful, like a fire that burns within or can explode in unreasonable rage. That rage can then lead to harmful acts that escalate a conflict to violence, which can lead others to fight back or to one getting caught and being convicted for criminal acts.

By contrast, if you can attach your anger to reason, although you might feel contempt or despise someone, you can rationally find the best time to attack strategically. This way you can hurt the other person without getting hurt yourself. Alternatively, you can find a way to let your anger go or find a creative outlet through which to release it.

Importantly, it helps to understand why you are angry, so you can overcome, tame, or redirect it. Otherwise, if you only let it go without this understanding, your anger might still come back.

Thus, there are many reasons to get one's anger under control, release it, push it down, and understand its source, so that reason, control, and making good choices will guide your actions. Then, once anger is combined with controlled reason, it can become a powerful force directed against others, such as when a lion or tiger lies in wait for the right time for a prey to come by, attack, and successfully make a kill.

The following quotes reflect this relationship between anger and reason.

"Anger is a wind which blows out the lamp of the mind."
Robert Green Ingersoll, American lawyer, political leader, 1833-1899

"No man can think clearly when his fists are clenched."
George Jean Nathan, American drama critic and editor, 1882-1958
Co-founder of *The American Mercury* and *The American Spectator*

"Anger is a short madness."
Horace, Roman poet, 65-8 BC

"Violence is the last refuge of the incompetent."
Isaac Asimov, American author, biochemistry professor, 1920-1992
Author or editor of over 500 sci-fi books

"Anger dwells only in the bosom of fools."
Albert Einstein, German-born theoretical physicist, 1879-1955
Developed the general theory of relativity

"Anger is never without an argument, but seldom with a good one."
George Savile, English statesman, writer, 1633-1695

"Keep cool; anger is not an argument."
Daniel Webster, American statesman, Congressman, 1782-1852

"Behind every argument is someone's ignorance."
Louis D. Brandeis, American lawyer, on Supreme Court , 1856-1941

"Arguments only confirm people in their own opinions."
Booth Tarkington, American novelist and dramatist, 1869-1946
Author of *The Magnificent Ambersons*

"Discussion is an exchange of knowledge; an argument is an exchange of ignorance."
Robert Quillen, American journalists and humorist, 1887-1948

"I am too weary to listen, too angry to hear."
Daniel Bell, American sociologist, writer, professor 1919-2011

"Hatred is an affair of the heart; contempt that of the head."
Arthur Schopenhauer, German philosopher 1788-1860

"Fair peace becomes men; ferocious anger belongs to beasts."
Ovid, Roman poet, 43 BC-17 AD

"Anger and intolerance are the enemies of correct understanding."
   Mahatma Gandhi, Indian independence movement leader, 1869-1948
   Inspired movement for civil rights and freedom across the world

"If you try to get rid of fear and anger without knowing their meaning, they will grow stronger and return."
   Deepak Chopra, Indian-Americn author, public speaker
   Author of *The Third Jesus: The Christ We Cannot Ignore*

"Anger based on calculated reason is more dangerous than anger based on blind hate."
   Richelle Mead, American fantasy writer
   Author of *Last Sacrifice*

ANGER AND OTHERS

What do you do when confronting others who are angry? Sometimes it works best to retreat from an emotional outburst of rage, rather than trying to respond in kind or with reason that may only further inflame the person who is angry. Then, after the person calms down, it can be feasible to approach him or her again and try to talk more reasonably to work things out.

On the other hand, it can be hard to deal with a person who is holding in his or her anger that might be unleashed when least expected. That's because the person who is seething underneath the surface is like a deadly snake in the grass, unseen and ready to strike when its target is most vulnerable and most likely to become a victim. Or perhaps the quietly angry person might be compared to a volcano, boiling within. Once triggered, it becomes deadly for all in its path.

You also have to be careful to whom you choose to express your anger, because of the consequences. Preferably avoid confronting a person who is more powerful or well-connected than you. Also be cautious about confronting a person who has much less than you, and so has little to risk in striking back. Or that person with much less could be full of anger, and your anger could provoke even more anger, much like tapping an anthill or beehive, only to be met by a swarm of angry ants or bees.

The following quotes suggest how to best deal with the anger of others.

"When you learn that a truth is a lie, anger follows."
Grace Slick, American singer-songwriter
Member of 1960s rock and roll band Jefferson Airplane

"Don't get mad, get even."
Robert F. Kennedy, American politician, 1925-1968

"Beware of him that is slow to anger; for when it is long coming, it is the stronger when it comes, and the longer kept. Abused patience turns to fury."
Frances Quarles, English poet, 1592-1644
Author of *Emblems*

"Quiet anger frightens me. The drunks, the idiots, the ones that rage easily – them I can handle. I know when to step out of their way. It's the ones that hold the anger in, the men that think about what they do and how they do it, that scare me. They're the ones that cause damage."
Katie McGarry, Young adult romance writer
Author of *Dare You To*

"Never contend with a man who has nothing to lose."
Baltasar Gracian, Spanish philosopher and writer, 1601-1658

"Never respond to an angry person with a fiery comeback, even if he deserves it…Don't allow his anger to become your anger."
Bohdi Sanders, writer, student of wisdom literature and martial arts
Author of *Warrior Wisdom: Ageless Wisdom for the Modern Warrior*

"Never be angry at something that can't get angry with you."
Jack Gardner, playwright, filmmaker, advertiser
Author of *Words Are Not Things*

"An angry player can't argue with the back of an umpire who is walking away."
Bill Klem, National League baseball umpire, 1874-1951

"The most dangerous irony is, people are angry with others because of their own incompetence."
Amit Kalantri, Indian writer
Author of *I Love You, Too* and *One Bucket of Tears*

"In some instances, you may care so much about the person who has hurt you, or be so unable to be angry with him (or with anyone), that you rationalize his hurtful acts by finding some basis in your own actions for his hurtful behavior; you then feel guilty rather than angry. Put in other terms, you become angry with yourself rather than with the one who hurt you."
Paul Ekman, American psychologist
Author of *Unmasking the Face: A Guide to Recognizing Emotions from Facial Cues*

ANGER, LOVE AND BETRAYAL

Two of the emotions or experiences that are especially likely to trigger anger are a love lost or a trust betrayed. Either can result in a very angry response, because these are such deeply held feelings, so when love or trust are damaged, this can lead to extreme rage.

For example, losing a love to a rival can provoke a great fury, because not only is the love lost, but that loss is due to the acts of another person. The rage can be even greater when that rival is a friend or close associate, for on top of losing that love, there are feelings of betrayal. No wonder the passion evoked runs so deep.

Another type of loss is being betrayed in business by a trusted partner or business associate, who has embezzled money or engaged in a power coup to take over the business. Likewise, in politics, the feelings of betrayal can be great, when a former associate turns against another and joins the opposition.

Whatever the reason for the loss or betrayal, the question is what to do about that resulting anger. Some choices and strategies for best controlling that anger that can result in a favorable outcome in the end, such as moving on to find success in another way. By contrast, an angry outburst might backfire and make the losses already suffered even worse.

The following quotes reflect the theme of feeling anger in response to problems of love and betrayal.

"The fiercest anger of all, the most incurable, is that which rages in the place of dearest love."
Euripedes, Athenian playwright and poet, 485-406 BC
Author of *Medea and Other Plays*

"Heaven has no rage like love to hatred turned, nor hell a fury like a woman scorned."
William Congreve, English playwright and poet, 1670-1729

"Sensitive people usually love deeply and hate deeply. They don't know any other way to live than by extremes because their emotional thermostat is broken."
Shannon L. Alder, , inspirational author
Wrote the most inspirational quotes on "Goodreads"
Author of *300 Questions to Ask Your Parents Before It's Too Late*

"If you let anger into your heart, it will push out your ability to love."
Bree Despain, American writer
Author of *The Dark Divine*

"A heart filled with anger has no room for love."
Joan Lunden, American journalist, TV host
Author of *Wake-Up Calls: Making the Most Out of Every Day*

"If you're angry at a loved one, hug that person. And mean it. You may not want to hug – which is all the more reason to do so. It's hard to stay angry when someone shows they love you, and that's precisely what happens when we hug each other."
Walter Anderson, Editor of *Parade Magazine*
Author of *The Confidence Course: Seven Steps to Self-Fulfillment*

WHEN ANGER BECOMES FUN

While anger is commonly viewed as a negative emotion that can be destructive or as a positive force contributing to survival or leading to change, anger can also be used, in a controlled way, just for fun.

One way it is fun is for spectators, who watch people go at it, such as in a boxing ring or other sports competitions, where anger can be a great motivator in firing up a competitor to win. Then, too, feuds between celebrities can be fun to watch, as the combatants throw insults, exchange blows, and sometimes melt down under the pressure.

Still another example of anger as a source of fun are the videos of angry clashes between individuals that get millions of views on Facebook and other social media platforms. They are fascinating and fun to watch, much like watching a train wreck or a volcano explode – as long as one is at a safe distance and not in danger.

Likewise, anger fuels much of the TV and film industry, whether the subject is a comedy, reality show, historical epic, or drama. At the heart of any story is conflict and resolving it in some way, and the trigger for much of this conflict is anger – whether directed at another person, oneself, or society as a whole.

In other words, anger is an emotion that not only is a survival mechanism, but it adds to the enjoyment of life. It stimulates and excites us; and without anger, life might be boring indeed. You can see the same dynamic in observing animals, who get angry at one another as well as humans.

So there's no getting away from anger, and besides being able to control it, you might enjoy it, too.

The follow quotes express this use of anger for enjoyment and fun.

"People are unjust to anger – it can be enlivening and a lot of fun."
Philip Roth, American novelist
Author of *Goodbye, Columbus*

"There are few more powerful ways of touching old sores than a good old, hilariously joyful bout of anger. All that unleashed passion, causing tsunamis of frustration: they're all guiding you straight to…the stuff that at - the heart of it - causes the outbursts in the first place."

Aernout Zevenbergen, journalist, author and speaker specializing in spirituality and self- development

"A rage can indeed be a ride on the back of a fiery dragon on steroids through the flames of hell, but as long as You (as in: your higher self, the 'noble part' of you) keep the reigns to the dragon that ride could be (and probably will be) one of the most liberating rides of your life."

Aernout Zevenbergen, journalist, author and speaker specializing in spirituality and self- development.

WHAT TO DO WHEN YOU OR SOMEONE ELSE IS ANGRY

Now that you've seen examples of how destructive and dangerous uncontrolled anger can be and the importance of releasing, taming, and letting go of anger, what can you do to handle your own anger, or know how to respond when someone else is expressing their anger to you? Here are some tips for dealing with anger generally.

Dealing with Your Anger in Resolving a Conflict

Should anger arise in a conflict situation, I have written a book called *Resolving Conflict*, which provides techniques for applying the E-R-I method for dealing with your anger that gives rise to or results from a conflict. In this model, the "E" stands for the emotions, the "R" for reason, and the "I" for the intuition. A first step in any conflict is to get rid of the negative emotions, including anger, which have triggered or resulted from the conflict, because it is hard to resolve anything when you or the other party or parties are emotional.

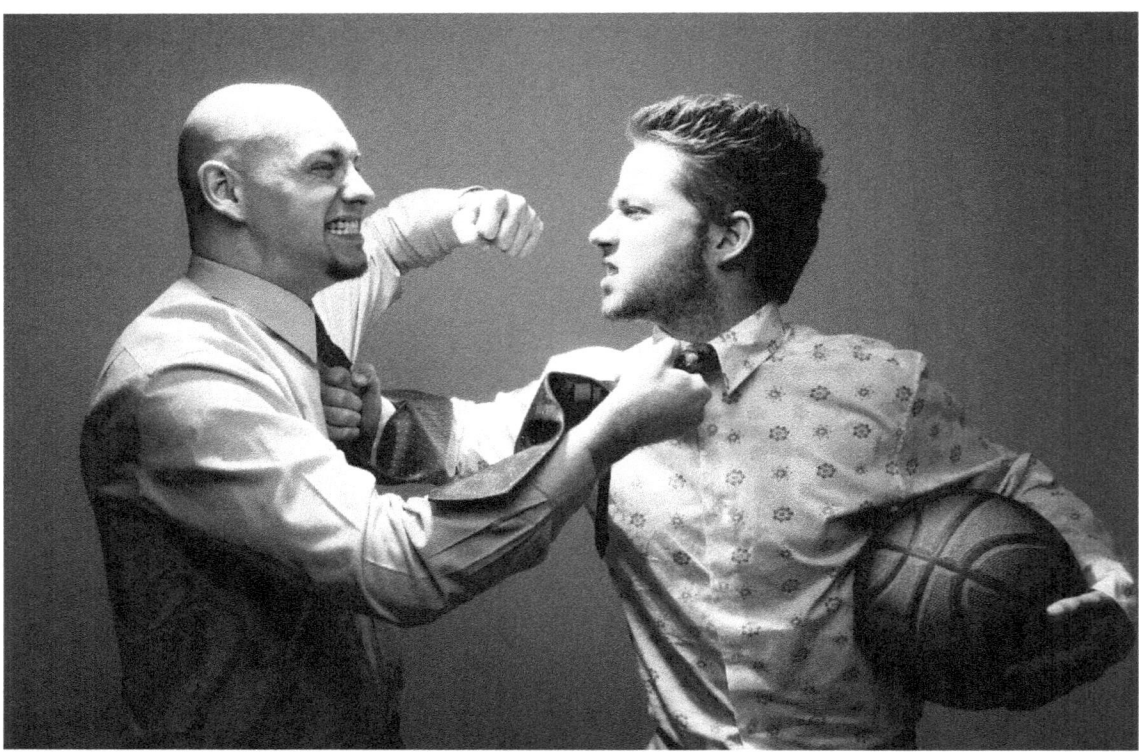

As a second step, consider the reasons that have led to this conflict and the different strategies for dealing with what occurred. This way you can choose the best approach, based on using a matrix for conflict resolution that includes the degree to which you assert yourself to deal with the other's concerns or your own concerns. Originally developed by Kenneth W. Thomas and Ralph H. Kilmann and known as the Thomas-Kilmann- Conflict Mode Instrument, this matrix features five basic strategies, though you can combine them in different ways. These include:

- <u>avoidance</u>, where you don't deal with the conflict at all; instead you might leave or delay, as a way to calm down and release your anger or that of the other party or parties;

- <u>accommodation</u>, where you go along with what the other person wants, which can be a good way to tamp down the other person's anger;

- <u>competition</u> or <u>confrontation</u>, where you go after what you want and even attack the other person because you are angry, which might be an effective strategy when you attack verbally, but can lead to violence if you don't control your anger;

- <u>collaboration</u>, where you take the time to discuss your differing concerns, which works best when you and the other party or parties can contain your anger rather than expressing it openly;

- <u>compromise</u>, where you each give a little to gain a little, so you reach an agreement that satisfies each party to some degree; you don't get everything you want, but in a good compromise, you get what's most important to you, just as the other party gains what is most important to him or her. In reaching such a compromise, you might contain your anger or express it in a calm, controlled way, so you show why this issue is important to you, but at the same show your willingness to work together to achieve a reasonable solution that works for all parties.

Other Ways to Deal with Your Anger

Whether or not your anger involves a conflict situation or occurs in your personal or work life, here are some general tips.

- Recognize and acknowledge your anger, since everyone gets angry at times, though the emotional experience can range from feeling a quiet burn to exploding with rage.

- Understand that feeling angry is a natural survival mechanism that is designed to protect you, such as in response to feelings that you were wronged in some way. So there is a truth to any feelings of anger, although they can be based on wrong information. Thus, it's important to look at the source of your anger and see if it is based on valid knowledge.

- Once you know the source of your anger, you can do something about it. If your anger is based on wrong information, your anger might naturally dissipate once you know the truth, such as if you are angry because you think a trusted friend or business associate betrayed you but discover this isn't true. Or if this information is valid, you can decide the best approach to deal with the situation, such as directing your anger into a positive response. For example, you might seek to correct an injustice in the system or find a way to quietly undermine a person who has treated you unfairly, without further hurting yourself.

- Realize that uncontrolled anger can be very destructive, so you want to control it. This control can involve choosing how to express it or not or choosing how to channel and direct your anger in positive and productive ways.

- When your response is to quietly simmer with anger, recognize that directing your anger inward can be destructive to you emotionally and mentally, as well as cause physical symptoms, such as ulcers. So you want to release or channel your anger away from yourself.

- When you choose to express your anger in what you say or do, you want to be able to tame it, so you don't erupt at the wrong time or place and hurt yourself by saying or doing things you later regret. In fact, this kind of open expression of anger is what can be the most dangerous, such as if you express your anger through road rage, attacking other people, or causing injury or even death. While, this might be a way to initially feel good and justified, such an attack can breed escalation and retaliation, and it can often end badly with your being hurt, arrested, or even dead.

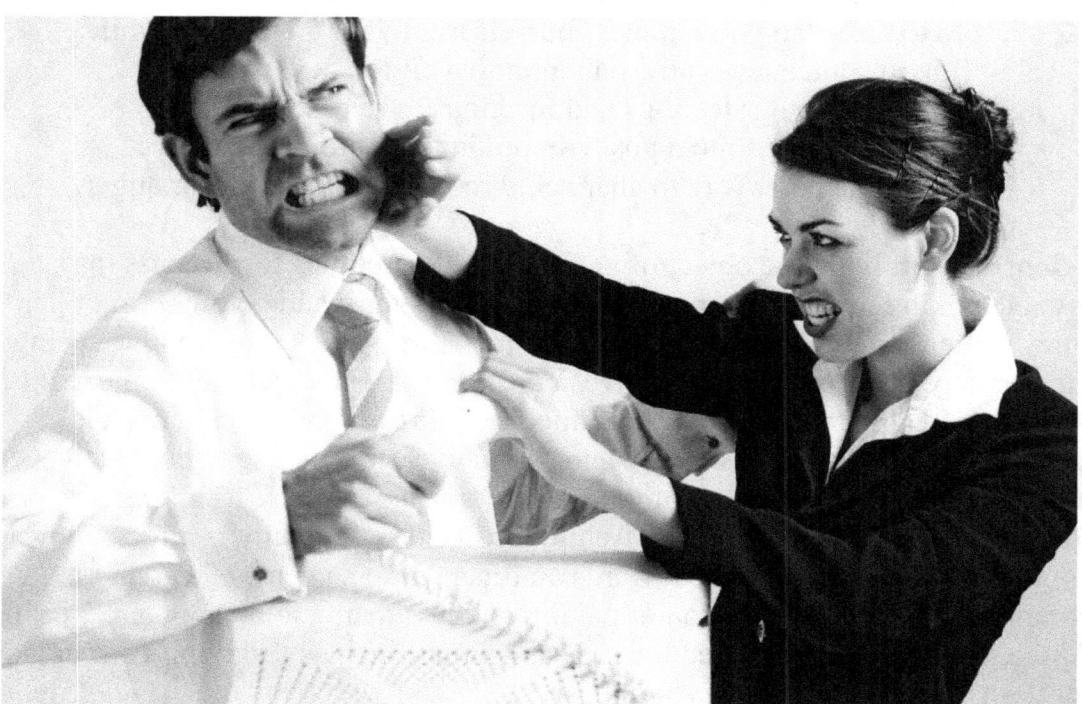

- Whatever you are angry about, think about how you can channel that anger into fixing things. For example:
	- If you are angry about yourself, consider how you might change or improve yourself, or correct a situation that has made you angry.
	- If you are angry at another person, think about the best way to respond or not, such as by avoiding that person, exposing that person without harming yourself, having a discussion to work out the problem, or redirecting your anger elsewhere, if this is a person of power you have to continue to deal with, such as a boss or leader of a social group.
	- If you are angry at a problem in the system, consider how you can avoid that problem in the future or how you might take some action yourself or with others to fix it.

- Consider the different choices you might have to deal with your anger. Aside from expressing it through words or actions, where you control what you say or do, you can find ways to release it to feel better. Some ways to let go are these:
	- Take time to relax, such as meditating or getting a massage to calm down.
	- Engage in an activity you like to direct your attention from your anger.
	- Go to sleep, so you remove yourself from your anger for a while.
	- Talk to someone you trust about how you feel.
	- Write down your feelings and reactions to release them.
	- Turn your anger into a positive, productive, profitable project.
	- Find some other way to channel, direct, and dissipate your anger.

- Consider forgiving the object of your anger. Sometimes forgiveness may involve talking to this person about why you are angry and getting him or her to show some remorse or contrition. Sometimes forgiveness may involve seeing that the person who wronged you receive some punishment or provide some restitution – whether negotiated by you or by someone acting on your behalf, such an attorney or the criminal justice system. Whatever you choose to do, forgiveness means emotionally letting go of your anger to that person by forgiving him or her for whatever he or she has done. While forgiveness generally is directed towards another person, it can also be towards an organization, such as forgiving a company for overcharging you or paying you less than you feel you are worth. And it might even be directed towards an animal, such as forgiving your dog or cat for destroying something in your house.

- To help you let go or forgive, think about what has made you angry from the point of view of the other party. Viewed from this perspective, you may understand or feel empathy for that person, because you understand why he said or acted as he did. In fact, often you may find your anger is based in miscommunication, where the other person has said or done things out of anger against you. So if you can clear up the misunderstanding, you can get rid of the anger – and end not only your own anger, but the other person's anger, too.

- Think about the ways that anger can lead to change in yourself, in the way you relate to others, in the way you do things or in your relationships with family members, relatives, friends, business associates, or with others in your neighborhood or community.

- Consider what fears could be triggering your anger, since often anger is a response to something you fear. But instead of becoming sad and afraid, you feel anger at yourself for being afraid or at the person, thing, or situation that is making you afraid. Then, that anger can lead you to strike out emotionally, instead of dealing with the underlying fear, and due to your fear, you may not strike out at what you fear, but at someone or something else. For example, you are afraid of your boss but feel helpless to do anything at work, so you take out your anger on your friends or family by yelling at them or storming out in a rage. But if you drill down to find your fear, you can deal with the real cause of your anger in a rational, calm, and productive way.

- Consider how your anger might be triggered by something you are trying to deny, such as true information about yourself or others you don't want to accept. For example, someone may tell you something negative you don't want to accept about someone you admire, so you become angry at the person telling you this information, not wanting to acknowledge the truth.

- Look for reasonable ways to direct or express your anger, since anger is often based on irrational thinking, triggered by the emotions. So after calming down and releasing your anger, look to your reason to come up with solutions. Your intuition might help you come up with ideas, such as through brainstorming. Later, your reason can help you decide on the best approach and the next steps to take now.

- Recognize that feelings of anger can become especially intense when feelings of love or experiences of betrayal by someone you trust are involved. That's because you already have an emotional connection with the other person. As a result, when they disappoint, leave, or betray you, you are more likely to feel any anger more intensely. In response, learn to do even more to control those feelings, since such anger is more likely to inspire intense negative feelings, such as jealousy, rage, and a burning desire for revenge, which might lead to irrational acts of passion that you will later regret or will bring you harm.

- Just as you might find forgiveness can help to heal your anger, so can seeking to replace your feelings of anger with feelings of love. In doing so, besides forgiving the person who has harmed you, you might also reach out to that person with love. However, do so carefully to be sure your good feelings will be reciprocated and the other person won't take advantage of your good nature. This approach of responding with love is advocated by many religions -- forgive and love the person who has wronged you. When you do, you may often find that person will reciprocate with appreciation and a desire to help and express love to you back. As some believe, "givers gain," and having this attitude can be a way to turn your anger into something positive, whereby you end up giving and then gaining back from the other person, instead of upping your anger toward that person and finding that he or she likewise continues to respond with anger towards you.

- In short, whenever you experience anger, see how you can learn from that anger and do what you need to do to protect yourself and deal with your underlying fears. Then, choose how to control and let go of your anger, while turning it into something positive to add more satisfaction and success to your life.

ANGER QUESTIONNAIRE

      The following questionnaire will help you think about your own anger issues and what to do about them. You can write in the spaces provided, or get some paper to create your own answer form.

1. What makes me angry? Write down the things that make you angry in the first column and what you can do about them in the second column. Think of as many possibilities as you want. Later you can determine what possibilities to act on and note the results.

What Makes Me Angry	What I Can Do About It

      Go back over your list, and rank the items from 1 to 5, based on what you think is most important to deal with first, second, third, or maybe not at all.

2. Is there anything I'm angry about where I need more information to better understand the situation? If so, what do I need to do, or who do I need to speak to, to better know what is really going on?

What Do I Need More Information About	What Can I Do to Get that Information

3. How can I let go of, channel, or redirect my anger into some other activity or project? Write down the things you might like to do.

4. For each thing you have listed that makes you angry, write down what it is and what

you can do about it. Later, write down what you actually did, with what results. Pick the top one or two items on your list to work on first.

What Makes Me Angry:_____

What I Can Do About It	What I Have Done	Results	How I Feel

5. Find a way to reward yourself for your achievement. Write down the ways you might

reward yourself or celebrate each time you achieve a goal.

PART II: DEALING WITH YOUR FEAR AND ANXIETY

INTRODUCTION TO PART II

When you encounter any kind of challenge, you may experience some fear and anxiety about the negative effects this situation may have on your life as well as concern about whether you can successfully master this challenge. You may also be anxious and fearful about how this situation is affecting others who are important in your life, as well as about your work or business.

Today, the level of fear and anxiety is especially high for everyone, because the pandemic caused by the coronavirus has transformed everyday interactions around the world. People fear sickness and death, so they are seeking ways to avoid this by hunkering down and avoiding social contact, which has been the lifeblood of society.

Much fear and anxiety is also due to the uncertainty and not knowing what will happen. As a result, people fear the unknown and our ability to overcome this new threat to our lives. Often they experience anxiety, a type of fear characterized by worry, nervousness, and unease, typically about an upcoming event or something with an uncertain outcome.

Such current fears reflect the many fears we confront as we go through life. So the wisdom on dealing with different types of fears over the ages is still applicable today. These insights can help calm you and motivate you to make good choices about what to do. Then, you can act accordingly.

To this end, the following quotes show the many ways you can understand and overcome your fears and anxieties whatever the cause. These quotes also illustrate how to more courageously and wisely act to overcome fears and face challenges.

THE DANGER OF FEAR

Fear can be a very protective emotion, since it alerts us to danger and keeps us safe. It leads us to respond with a fight or flight response to this perception of danger.

Any fear can be destructive in causing us to hold back from meeting a challenge or acting to achieve a desired goal. Such a fear can lead us to think we are not worthy or don't have the ability to confront and overcome an obstacle. It can lead us to separate ourselves from others, because we fear those we should trust. It can lead us to retreat when we should move forward. That's why some commentators have called fear the most dangerous emotion or said that the biggest danger comes from being afraid.

Thus, it is important to seek to have no fear or to attack and destroy it, once we feel fear.

Following are some quotes from individuals talking about our biggest fears, the source of fear, and how our fears can separate us from others.

The Biggest Fear

The only thing we have to fear is fear itself."
Franklin D. Roosevelt, 32nd President of the United States, 1882-1945.

"The oldest and strongest emotion of mankind is fear, and the oldest and strongest kind of fear is fear of the unknown."
H. P. Lovecraft, American writer with a focus on horror fiction, 1890-1937.

"Fear defeats more people than any other one thing in the world."
Ralph Waldo Emerson, American essayist and lecturer, 1803-1882.

"There is no greater hell than to be a prisoner of fear."
Ben Jonson, English playwright, poet, actor, and literary critic. 1572-1637.

The Source of Fear

"Fear is an insidious and deadly thing. It can warp judgment, freeze reflexes, breed mistakes. Worse, it's contagious."
Jimmy Stewart, American actor and military officer, 1908-1997.

"Fear is pain arising from the anticipation of evil."
Aristotle, ancient Greek philosopher and scientist, 384 BC – 322 BC.

"Fear comes from uncertainty. When we are absolutely certain, whether of our worth or worthlessness, we are almost impervious to fear."
William Congreve, English playwright and poet, 1670-1729.

"The deepest fear we have, 'the fear beneath all fears,' is the fear of not measuring up, the fear of judgment. It's this fear that creates the stress and depression of everyday life."
Tullian Tchividjian, former pastor of the Presbyterian Church in America denomination, 1972-present.

Fear of Others

"The enemy is fear. We think it is hate; but, it is fear."
Gandhi, Indian activist and leader of the Indian independence movement,. 1869-1948.

"Fear is the most debilitating emotion in the world, and it can keep you from ever truly knowing yourself and others - its adverse effects can no longer be overlooked or underestimated. Fear breeds hatred, and hatred has the power to destroy everything in its path."
Kevyn Aucoin, American make-up artist, photographer, and author, 1962-2002.

"Fear makes strangers of people who would be friends."
Shirley MacLaine, American film, television, and theater actress, 1934-present.

CONQUERING AND OVERCOMING FEAR

In response to fears and anxiety, many commentators talk about conquering, confronting, or overcoming these emotions in various ways. They speak of being fearless, avoiding worry about the future, overcoming uncertainty, and gaining wisdom when you conquer fear. They urge you to resist or attack fear, sometimes by simply letting it go. You should also be self-reliant, and have no regrets when you act. Perhaps you can even have fun as a way to escape your fears.

Following are some quotes from individuals talking about confronting, conquering, or overcoming fear.

Being Fearless

"You gain strength, courage, and confidence by every experience in which you really stop to look fear in the face. You are able to say to yourself, 'I lived through this horror. I can take the next thing that comes along.'"
Eleanor Roosevelt, former First Lady of the United States from March 1933 to April 1945, 1884-1962.

"The secret of life is to have no fear; it's the only way to function."
Stokely Carmichael, Trinidad-born organizer in the Civil Rights Movement, 1941-1998.

"Nothing in the affairs of men is worthy of great anxiety."
Plato, ancient Greek Philosopher and founder of the Academy in Athens, 428 BC – 384 BC.

Avoiding Worry about the Future

"What else does anxiety about the future bring you but sorrow upon sorrow?"
Thomas A Kempis, German-Dutch canon regular. Author of *The Imitation of Christ,* 1380-1471.

"I am not afraid of tomorrow, for I have seen yesterday and I love today."
William Allen White, American newspaper editor, politician, author, and leader of the Progressive Movement. 1868-1944.

"Fear keeps us focused on the past or worried about the future. If we can acknowledge our fear, we can realize that right now we are okay. Right now, today, we are still alive, and our bodies are working marvelously. Our eyes can still see the beautiful sky. Our ears can still hear the voices of our loved ones."
Thich Nhat Hanh, Vietnamese Buddhist monk and peace activist, 1926-present.

Overcoming Uncertainty

"Fear is often our immediate response to uncertainty. There's nothing wrong with experiencing fear. The key is not to get stuck in it."
Gabrielle Bernstein, American motivational speaker, life coach, and author, 1979-present.

"Fear is like a black cavern that is terrifying. Once you enter the cavern and explore it, you realize that you can get out of it, go through it and get out of it."
Isabel Allende, Chilean writer, 1942-present.

Gaining Wisdom

"To conquer fear is the beginning of wisdom."
Bertrand Russell, British philosopher, logician, mathematician, historian, and Nobel Laureate, 1872-1970.

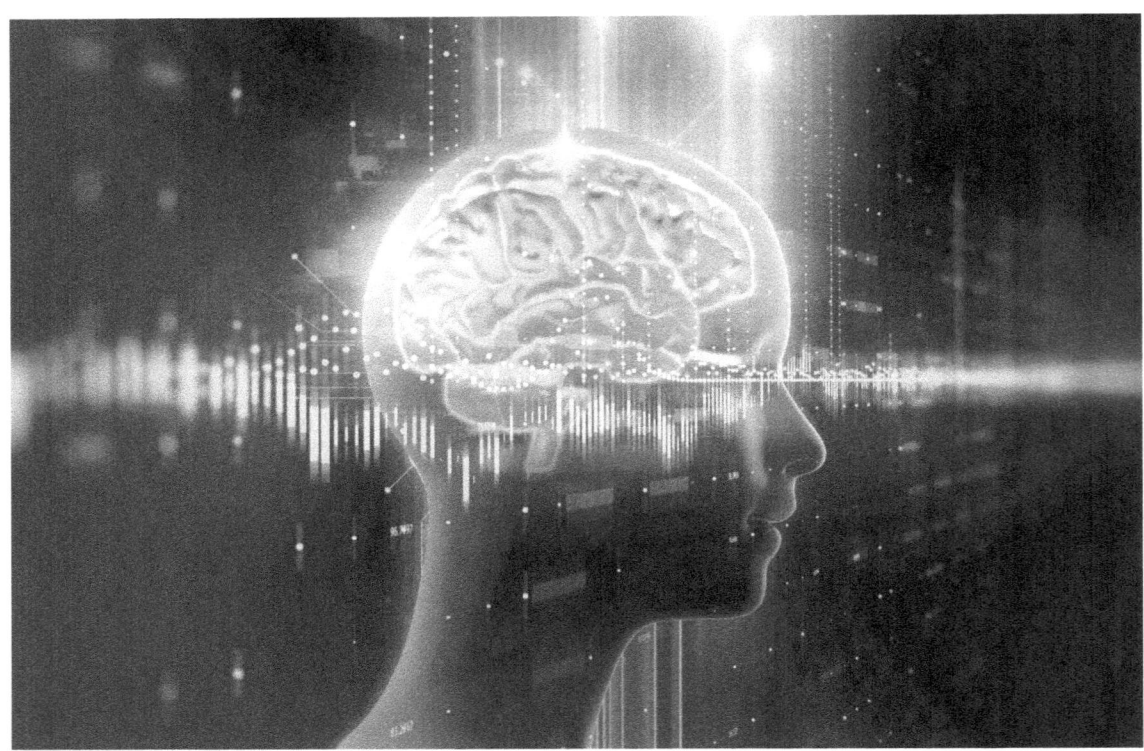

Resisting or Attacking Fear

"Resist your fear; fear will never lead to you a positive end. Go for your faith and what you believe."
T. D. Jakes, American pastor, author, and filmmaker, 1957-present.

"As soon as the fear approaches near, attack and destroy it."
Chanakya, Indian teacher, philosopher, jurist, and royal advisor, 371 BC – 283 BC

"The key to change... is to let go of fear."
Rosanne Cash, American singer-songwriter and author, 1955-present.

"Write down everything you fear in life. Burn it. Pour herbal oil with a sweet scent on the ashes."
Yoko Ono, Japanese multimedia artist, singer, songwriter, and peace activist, 1933-present.

Being Self-Reliant

"The whole secret of existence is to have no fear. Never fear what will become of you, depend on no one. Only the moment you reject all help are you freed."
Swami Vivekananda, Indian Hindu monk, and chief disciple of Ramakrishna, 1863-1902.

Having No Regrets

"Fear is stupid. So are regrets."
Marilyn Monroe, American actress, model, and singer, 1926-1962.

Having Fun

"There's no fear when you're having fun."
Will Thomas, American novelist. Known for his Victorian mystery series featuring Cyrus Barker, 1958-present.

HAVING COURAGE

Another way to deal with a fear is to have courage in order to conquer or overcome it. Such courage enables you to resist and master fear, even if you are initially fearful.

Being courageous also involves disregarding any fears and acting anyway. Doing what you fear can also lead you to break through your comfort zone and gain strength, confidence, and a feeling of power for discovering that you can do what you fear. That can lead to you live a more fulfilling life. Moreover, your courage can be an inspiration to others, and having faith will help you face and overcome your fears.

Following are some quotes from individuals talking about the importance of having courage in the face of fear.

Being Courageous and Unafraid

"America was not built on fear. America was built on courage, on imagination and an unbeatable determination to do the job at hand."
Harry S Truman, 33rd President of the United States, 1884-1972.

"Life shrinks or expands in proportion to one's courage."
Anais Nin, French-American diarist, essayist, novelist, 1903-1977.

"The first and great commandment is: Don't let them scare you."
Elmer Davis, news reporter, author, and the Director of the United States Office of War Information during World War II, 1890-1958.

"Without fear there cannot be courage."
Christopher Paolini, American writer. Author of *Eragon, Eldest, Brisingr,* and *Inheritance,* 1983-present.

"None but a coward dares to boast that he has never known fear."
Bertrand Russell, British philosopher, logician, mathematician, historian, writer, social critic, political activist, and Nobel laureate, 1872-1970.

"Here is the world. Beautiful and terrible things will happen. Don't be afraid."
Frederick Buechner, American writer, novelist, poet, preacher, and essayist.

"Only when we are no longer afraid do we begin to live."
Dorothy Thompson, American journalist and radio broadcaster, 1893-1961.

"Fear has its use but cowardice has none."
Mahatma Gandhi, Indian activist and leader of the Indian independence movement, 1869-1948.

Resisting and Overcoming Fear

"Courage is resistance to fear, mastery of fear, not absence of fear."
Mark Twain, pen name for Samuel Langhorne Clemens. American writer and humorist known for *The Adventures of Tom Sawyer* and *Adventures of Huckleberry Finn,*
1835-1910.

"I learned that courage was not the absence of fear, but the triumph over it. The brave man is not he who does not feel afraid, but he who conquers that fear."
Nelson Mandela, President of South Africa, anti-apartheid revolutionary and political leader, 1918-2013.

"Use your fear... it can take you to the place where you store your courage.
Amelia Earhart, American aviation pioneer and author. First female aviator to fly solo across the Atlantic Ocean, 1897-1939.

"Kill the snake of doubt in your soul, crush the worms of fear in your heart and mountains will move out of your way."
Kate Seredy, Hungarian writer and illustrator of children's books. 1899-1975.

Taking Action Despite your Fears

"Scared is what you're feeling. Brave is what you're doing."
Emma Donoghue, Irish-Canadian playwright, literary historian, novelist, and screenwriter. Author of *Room*, 1969-present.

"Courage is being scared to death…and saddling up anyway."
John Wayne, nicknamed "The Duke," an American actor, filmmaker, and Academy Award-winner for the 1969 *True Grit*, 1907–1979.

"Courage is doing what you're afraid to do. There can be no courage unless you're scared."
Eddie Rickenbacker, an American fighter ace in World War I and a Medal of Honor recipient, 1890-1973.

"Bravery is the capacity to perform properly even when scared half to death."
Omar N. Bradley, a senior officer of the United States Army during and after World War II, 1893-1981.

"Courage is fear holding on a minute longer."
George S. Patton, general in the United States Army, 1885-1945.

"The greatest mistake you can make in life is continually fearing that you'll make one."
Elbert Hubbard, American writer, publisher, artist, and philosopher, 1856-1915.

"Bravery does not mean being fearless. It means to be full of fear but still not being dominated by it."
Rajneesh, Indian mystic and leader of the Rajneesh movement, 1931-1990.

Gaining Strength, Confidence, and Power by Doing What You Fear

"If it scares you, it might be a good thing to try."
Seth Godin, American author of 17 business success books, 1960-present.

"To uncover your true potential, you must first find your own limits and then you have to have the courage to blow past them."
Picabo Street, an American former World Cup alpine ski racer and Olympic gold medalist, 1971-present.

"We gain strength, and courage, and confidence by each experience in which we really stop to look fear in the face... we must do that which we think we cannot."
Eleanor Roosevelt, former First Lady of the United States, American political figure, diplomat, and activist, 1884-1962.

Overcoming Adversity and Difficulties

"We don't develop courage by being happy every day. We develop it by surviving difficult times and challenging adversity."
Barbara De Angelis, American relationship consultant, lecturer, and author, 1951-present.

"You must learn to be strong in the dark as well as in the day, else you will always be only half brave."
George MacDonald, Scottish author, poet, and Christian minister, 1824-1905.

"Do not pray for an easy life, pray for the strength to endure a difficult one"
Bruce Lee, Hong Kong and American actor, film director, martial artist, and founder of Jeet Kune Do, 1940-1973.

"Great crisis produce great men and great deeds of courage."
John F Kennedy, an American politician and 35th President of the United States from 1961 until he was assassinated in November 1963, 1917-1963.

Living a More Fulfilling Life

"Life shrinks or expands in proportion to one's courage."
Anais Nin, French-American diarist, essayist, and novelist, 1903-1977.

"What would life be if we had no courage to attempt anything?"
Vincent Van Gogh, Dutch Post-Impressionist painter, known for "The Starry Night," 1853-1890.

"I need to put myself out in the world and be brave and be uncomfortable. When I do, it means I can enjoy life so much more."
Annabelle Wallis, an English actress, known for playing Jane Seymour in Showtime's period drama *The Tudors* from 2009 to 2010.

"It takes courage to grow up and become who you really are."
e.e. Cummings, a poet, painter, essayist, author, and playwright, who wrote approximately 2900 poems, 1894-1962.

"If you are lucky enough to find a way of life you love, you have to find the courage to live it."
John Irving, American novelist and screenwriter, 1942-present.

Inspiring Others

"Keep your fears to yourself, but share your courage with others."
Robert Louis Stevenson, Scottish novelist, poet, essayist, musician, and travel writer. Author of *Treasure Island* and *The Strange Case of Dr. Jekyll and Mr. Hyde*, 1850-1894.

"Courage is contagious. When a brave man takes a stand, the spines of others are often stiffened."
Billy Graham, American evangelist and ordained Southern Baptist minister, 1918-2018.

DO IT ANYWAY

Another way to deal with your fears is to take action by trying something new and acting in spite of your fears. Do what you fear or what makes you anxious. Just taking some action, any action, will help to redirect your mind away from your concerns and worries. Such action can help you gain new opportunities and achieve your dreams, though these actions can mean taking risks. Still, you should choose to do what you want rather than just doing what is safe. The result can be feeling a new sense of freedom.

In other words, "Do it now!" and you will overcome your fear or fears.

Following are some quotes from individuals talking about taking action, despite being fearful, in order to overcome fear.

Trying New Things

"Don't let fear or insecurity stop you from trying new things. Believe in yourself. Do what you love. And most importantly, be kind to others, even if you don't like them."
Stacy London, American fashion consultant, author, and magazine editor 1969-present.

"I've learned that fear limits you and your vision. It serves as blinders to what may be just a few steps down the road for you. The journey is valuable, but believing in your talents, your abilities, and your self-worth can empower you to walk down an even brighter path. Transforming fear into freedom - how great is that?"
Soledad O'Brien, American broadcast journalist and executive producer 1966-present.

"Slowness to change usually means fear of the new."
Phil Crosby, American actor and singer, 1934-2004.

"Curiosity will conquer fear even more than bravery will."
James Stephens, American television actor, 1951-present.

Acting in Spite of Your Fear

The Bible says to 'fear not,' but this doesn't mean you should never feel scared. It means when you do feel fear, keep going forward and do what you are supposed to do. Or as I like to say, do it afraid."
Joyce Meyer, American author and president of Joyce Meyer Ministries. 1943-present.

"I am totally fearless! Well, of course, I'm not totally fearless. I worry constantly and obsess over things, but I just don't let fear stand in the way of doing something that I really want to do."
Tom Ford, American fashion designer, film director, screenwriter, and film producer, 1961-present.

"Find out what you're afraid of and go live there."
Chuck Palahniuk, American novelist and freelance journalist, 1962-present.

Acting to Overcome Your Fears

"Thinking will not overcome fear but action will."
W. Clement Stone, American businessman and philanthropist, 1902-2002.

"Do one thing every day that scares you."
Eleanor Roosevelt, former First Lady of the United States from March 1933 to April 1945, 1884-1962.

"Action cures fear, inaction creates terror."
Douglas Horton, American Protestant clergyman and academic leader, 1891-1968.

"If you want to conquer fear, don't sit home and think about it. Go out and get busy."
Dale Carnegie, American writer and developer of courses in self-improvement, 1888-1955.

"Do the thing you fear most and the death of fear is certain."
Mark Twain, pen name for Samuel Langhorne Clemens. American writer and humorist, 1835-1910.

"You can't let fear paralyze you. The worse that can happen is you fail, but guess what: You get up and try again. Feel that pain, get over it, get up, dust yourself off and keep it moving."
Queen Latifah, American rapper, songwriter, singer, actress, and producer, 1970-present.

Being Willing to Take Risks

"Living with fear stops us taking risks, and if you don't go out on the branch, you're never going to get the best fruit."
Sarah Parish, English actress. Known for her work on *The Pillars of the Earth,* 1968-present.

"Avoiding danger is no safer in the long run than outright exposure. The fearful are caught as often as the bold."
Helen Keller, American author, political activist, and lecturer. First deaf-blind person to earn a bachelor of arts degree, 1880-1968.

Achieving What You Want by Doing What You Fear

"The cave you fear to enter holds the treasure you seek."
Joseph Campbell, American Professor of Literature at Sarah Lawrence College, 1904-1987.

"Everything you want is on the other side of fear."
Jack Canfield, American author, motivational speaker, and entrepreneur. Co-author of the *Chicken Soup for the Soul* series, 1944-present.

"Fear has two meanings: 'Forget Everything And Run' or 'Face Everything And Rise.' The choice is yours."
Zig Ziglar, American author, salesman, and motivational speaker, 1926-2012.

"Every journey starts with fear."
Jake Gyllenhaal, American actor, 1980-present.

"I'm not afraid of storms, for I'm learning how to sail my ship."
Louisa May Alcott, American novelist and poet. Author of *Little Women*. 1832-1888.

Choosing What You Want, Not What Is Safe

"Eighty percent of all choices are based on fear. Most people don't choose what they want; they choose what they think is safe."
Phil McGraw, American television personality and psychologist. Host of the television show Dr. Phil, 1950-present.

"You always have two choices: your commitment versus your fear."
Sammy Davis, Jr., American singer, musician, dancer, actor, 1925-1990.

"Too many people are thinking of security instead of opportunity. They seem to be more afraid of life than death."
James F. Byrnes, American judge and politician from South Carolina. Served in Congress, executive branch, and on the United States Supreme Court, 1882-1972.

"Fear is the foundation of safety."
Tertullian, prolific Christian author, 160 - 220.

Feeling Free By Acting

"Expose yourself to your deepest fear; after that, fear has no power, and the fear of freedom shrinks and vanishes. You are free."
Jim Morrison, American singer-songwriter. Lead vocalist of the Doors, 1943-1971.

"Ultimately we know deeply that the other side of every fear is freedom."
Mary Ferguson, Irish author and biographer., 1823-1905.

"I'll tell you what freedom is to me: no fear. I mean really, no fear!"
Nina Simone, American singer, songwriter, pianist, and activist in the Civil Rights Movement, 1933-2003.

"Anxiety is the dizziness of freedom."
Soren Kierkegaard, Danish philosopher, theologian, poet, and social critic 1813-1855.

Gaining Opportunities and Dreams

"Too many of us are not living our dreams because we are living our fears."
Les Brown, American motivational speaker, author, radio DJ, and former member of the Ohio House of Representatives, 1945-present.

"There is only one thing that makes a dream impossible to achieve: the fear of failure."
Paulo Coelho, Brazilian lyricist and novelist. Author of *The Alchemist*, 1947-present.

"I wish for a world where everyone understands that discomfort is the price of legendary. And fear is just growth coming to get you."
Robin S. Sharma, Canadian writer and motivational speaker. Author of *The Monk Who Sold His Ferrari* series, 1964-present.

"I believe that every single event in life happens in an opportunity to choose love over fear."
Oprah Winfrey, American media proprietor and talk show host, 1954-present.

"Fear doesn't enter into my vocabulary. Fear is the gateway to the next step in my development."
Catherine Oxenberg, American-Serbian actress and daughter of Princess Elizabeth of Yugoslavia, 1961-present.

UNDERSTANDING FEAR AND CHANGING YOUR MINDSET

It can help you deal with your fears, if you better understand their cause and recognize that how you experience fear and react to it is affected by your mindset. In turn, the knowledge you gain by paying attention to what is true will help you know what to do to overcome your fears.

Following are some quotes from individuals talking about how understanding your fears can help you better deal with what you fear and move on.

Recognizing Fear as a Mind Set

"Fears are nothing more than a state of mind."
Napoleon Hill, American self-help writer. Author of *Think and Grow Rich*. 1883-1970.

"Fear doesn't exist anywhere except in the mind."
Dale Carnegie, American writer and developer of courses in self-improvement, 1888-1955.

"Men are not afraid of things, but of how they view them."
Epictetus, Greek Stoic philosopher, 50-135.

"Fear is only as deep as the mind allows."
Japanese Proverb

"Fears are educated into us, and can, if we wish, be educated out."
Karl Augustus Menninger, American psychiatrist and part of the Menninger Foundation, 1893-1990.

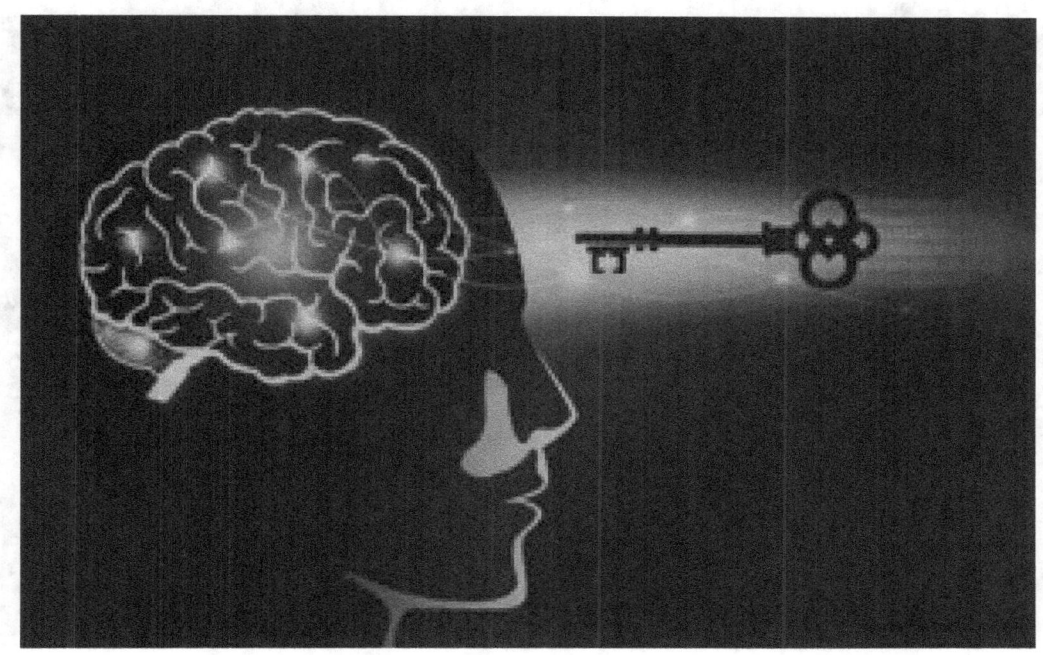

Gaining Knowledge to Overcome Fears

"Listen to what you know instead of what you fear."
Richard Bach, American writer. Author of *Jonathan Livingston Seagull* and *Illusions: The Adventures of a Reluctant Messiah,* 1936-present.

"Ignorance is the parent of fear."
Herman Melville, American novelist. Author of *Typee* and *Moby-Dick,* 1819-1891.

"No passion so effectually robs the mind of all its powers of acting and reasoning as fear."
Edmund Burke, Anglo-Irish statesman, 1729-1797.

"Nothing in life is to be feared, it is only to be understood. Now is the time to understand more, so that we may fear less."
Marie Curie, French-Polish physicist and chemist. Known for her research on radioactivity, 1867-1934.

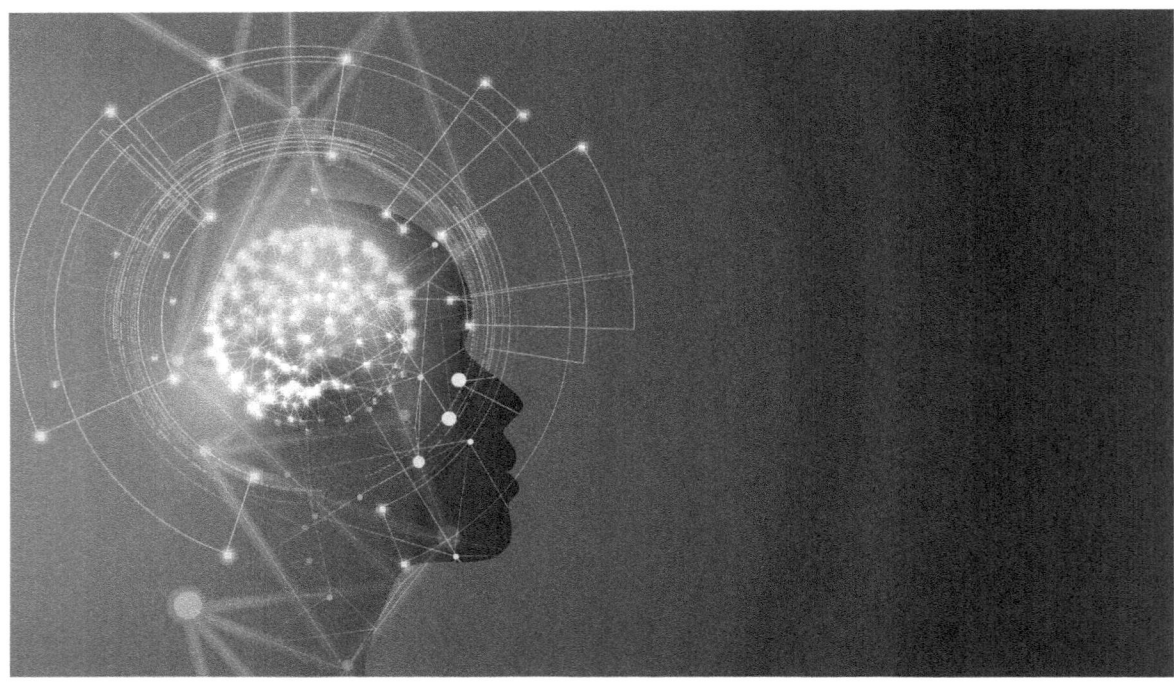

Understanding, Assessing, Controlling, and Managing Your Fear

"Courage is not the absence of fear, but rather the assessment that something else is more important than fear."
Franklin D. Roosevelt, 32nd President of the United States, American statesman, and political leader, 1882-1945.

"Courage is a special kind of knowledge: the knowledge of how to fear what ought to be feared and how not to fear what ought not to be feared."
David Ben-Gurion, the primary founder of the State of Israel and its first Prime Minister, 1886-1973.

"Courage is knowing what not to fear."
Plato, a philosopher in Classical Greece and the founder of the Academy in Athens, the first institution of higher learning in the Western world, 428–348 BC.

Paying Attention to What Is True

"The time to take counsel of your fears is before you make an important battle decision. That's the time to listen to every fear you can imagine! When you have collected all the facts and fears and made your decision, turn off all your fears and go ahead!"
George S. Patton, senior officer of the United States Army, 1885-1945.
"Fear: False Evidence Appearing Real." — Unknown

"Concentration is a fine antidote to anxiety."
Jack Nicklaus, American professional golfer. 1940-present.

"We are more often frightened than hurt; and we suffer more from imagination than from reality."
Seneca, Roman Stoic philosopher, statesman, and dramatist, 4 BC – 65.

Knowing What to Do

"I have learned over the years that when one's mind is made up, this diminishes fear; knowing what must be done does away with fear."

Rosa Parks, American activist in the Civil Rights Movement. Known for her role in the Montgomery Bus Boycott, 1913-2005.

TECHNIQUES FOR OVERCOMING YOUR FEARS

As the previous chapters have described, understanding and overcoming your fear can contribute to your achieving more success, happiness, and satisfaction in life. Like other qualities, such as courage, forgiveness and gratitude, overcoming your fears can contribute to better relationships with others and bring you more peace and contentment. Importantly, understanding your fears can help you overcome them and move on to bigger and better things.

Here are some things you can do to have more courage.

1) Keep a journal or add a section to your journal where you write down what you feel you need to do to overcome your fears. After you make your list, review each item and imagine yourself having the power to face each one. If it's a long list, prioritize what you want to do and tackle one or two items at a time. Imagine you are overcoming any fears and mastering any challenge. See yourself achieving a goal or being praised for your ability to confront and overcome your fears. As you imagine these experiences, feel yourself becoming stronger and more powerful, because you had ability to put aside your fear to do whatever you initially felt unsure about doing.

2) Make a list of 5 to 10 ways in which you have confronted your fears in the past and 5 to 10 things where you can show this ability in the future. Notice if there are any patterns on the lists, like certain types of situations where you have felt fear and have overcome that fear. Then, take some time to experience in your imagination those situations where you have overcome your fears. Next imagine yourself overcoming something you fear in a future situation. Experience a sense of peacefulness, freedom, power, satisfaction or other positive feelings as a result of what you have done or expect to do.

3) Write up your favorite quotes about understanding and dealing with fears using large fonts on separate sheets of paper. Post the quotes around your house where you can see them each day.

4) Take an overcoming fear walk around your neighborhood or nearby park. Think about all the times you have overcome a fear and what you need to confront a particular fear you have now. Feel a sense of power or freedom as you imagine each time you have overcome a fear the past or expect to experience it in the future. Try projecting your feelings of power on overcoming fear onto a bird you see nearby. When the bird flies, imagine you are soaring with the feelings of power or freedom that comes from confronting and overcoming a fear.

5) Pair up with a friend or business associate and take 5-10 minutes to talk about how you have confronted overcome a fear in the past week or what you need to do to overcome a current fear. Or form a weekly or monthly overcoming fear group of 3-10 people, where you share with one another for about an hour about your experiences of overcoming your fears for that past week or month.

6) Create a Vision Board or Vision Board Book, in which you gather images of situations in which you have confronted or overcome a fear or need to do so in the future. Then, paste these images on your board or in your book. Later, hang the Vision Board on a wall in your house or carry your Vision Board Book with you. You can look at these images from time to time to remind yourself to feel the sense of power and freedom that comes from confronting and overcoming your fears.

7) Create a list of 5-10 people who have done something to confront or overcome a fear and think about what they did. Notice if there are any patterns in the types of situations where they did this, so you can be learn from their experience and be even more confident in confronting and overcoming your own fears in the future.

8) Do a meditation on overcoming fear for 10-15 minutes on your own or with others. During this time, get relaxed, close your eyes, visualize what you have done to confront or overcome a fear, and feel that sense of power and freedom that comes from doing so.

9) If you experience difficulty in confronting or overcoming a fear, take some time to think about the reasons for this. If needed, discuss this difficulty with others who are working on being more fearless. Or remind yourself how your determination or courage has helped you overcome a fear, so you can feel more confident and powerful in what you can do in the future. Also, remind yourself of any successes you experienced after having the strength to do something you initially felt afraid to do. Reminding yourself of your past successes in overcoming a fear can help you be more successful in acting in the future to achieve your goals, despite any fears or challenges you face.

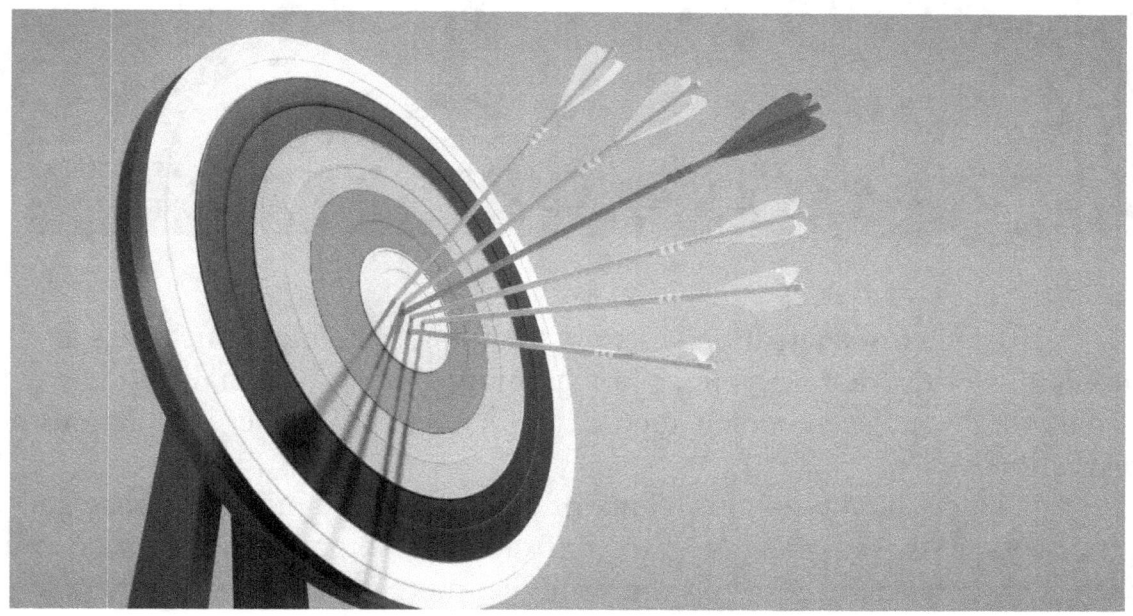

10) Think of a situation where in the future you might push pass any limitations or restrictions you feel are holding you back. Then, imagine what you might do and see yourself succeeding in overcoming these limitations or restrictions.

11) Now it's up to you. Think of other ways you might embrace and express your strength and power to confront and overcome any fears, so you can gain whatever success you want and feel more confidence, freedom, and power.

PART III: TAPPING INTO YOUR COURAGE

INTRODUCTION TO PART III

When you are facing any challenge, especially one that is very difficult or dangerous, courage can help you be strong and prevail. Courage has long been valued and honored as a virtue. It is commonly associated with acts of bravery, such as in a war or if someone does something daring and risky. The risk could be almost anything, from climbing a sheer mountain cliff or taking a leap of faith to engage in an uncertain business deal.

Courage is also seen as a needed quality to overcome a major challenge in life, such as to fight a dreaded disease or to succeed despite a disability. Additionally, one may need courage to break through a limiting belief or barrier in order to achieve greatness. Or one may need this quality to stand alone against others who have a different opinion or may be an enemy.

When courage leads to success, one can be richly rewarded, and when it doesn't, someone can be honored for what they tried to do against great odds. An example is awarding a medal of honor to a soldier who died in battle while saving his companions. Another example is praising the bravery of a person who jumps into the rapids to save someone from drowning at the risk of their own life. In politics, numerous examples of courageous leaders abound, such as those honored in John F. Kennedy's book *Profiles in Courage* and the tribute paid to Senator John McCain after his death for his repeated acts of courage. Most notably, McCain refused to be released as a prisoner of war while his fellow soldiers remained captives.

Then, too, courage is often associated with other virtues, such as freedom and independence, in that a courageous person can feel free of constraints in making choices based on personal values, rather than following the herd.

The following quotes show the many ways that courage is considered a valuable quality to have. They also illustrate how we can more courageously and wisely act to overcome fears and face challenges, despite the odds of potential failure, danger, or death. The quotes are organized by the different aspects of courage and include the name of the person first credited with that quote.

OVERCOMING FEAR

Courage is often associated with facing and overcoming fear. Being courageous involves quieting or disregarding any fears and acting with courage anyway. By doing so, one is considered brave or acting with valor, and often such bravery is honored, because one has done what others have been afraid to do.

For example, firefighters who take on raging fire or divers who make dangerous rescues are considered courageous. And many heroes in films and TV series, like Superman, Spiderman, and Batman, are watched avidly as they encounter one fear-inspiring challenge after another, before they ultimately prevail. Such heroes appear fearless or they accept each mission to save others from danger despite any fears they have. The basic theme of these films and TV shows is that this power over fear, reflected in these super heroes, will ultimately lead to a happy ending.

Doing what you fear can also lead you to break through your comfort zone and gain strength, confidence, and a feeling of empowerment for discovering that you can do what you fear, leading to your success. Moreover, your courage can inspire others, and having faith will help you face and overcome your fears.

Following are some quotes from individuals talking about this close relationship of courage and overcoming fear.

Facing everyday life without fear

"Here is the world. Beautiful and terrible things will happen. Don't be afraid."
Frederick Buechner, American writer, novelist, poet, preacher, and essayist.

Resisting, overcoming fear

"Courage is resistance to fear, mastery of fear, not absence of fear."
Mark Twain, pen name for Samuel Langhorne Clemens. American writer and humorist known for *The Adventures of Tom Sawyer* and *Adventures of Huckleberry Finn*, 1835-1910.

"I learned that courage was not the absence of fear, but the triumph over it. The brave man is not he who does not feel afraid, but he who conquers that fear."
Nelson Mandela, President of South Africa, anti-apartheid revolutionary and political leader, 1918-2013.

"Use your fear... it can take you to the place where you store your courage.
Amelia Earhart, American aviation pioneer and author. First female aviator to fly solo across the Atlantic Ocean, 1897-1939.

Taking action despite your fears

"Scared is what you're feeling. Brave is what you're doing."
Emma Donoghue, Irish-Canadian playwright, literary historian, novelist, and screenwriter. Author of *Room*.

"Courage is being scared to death…and saddling up anyway."
John Wayne, nicknamed "The Duke," an American actor, filmmaker, and Academy Award-winner for the 1969 *True Grit*, 1907–1979.

"Courage is doing what you're afraid to do. There can be no courage unless you're scared."
Eddie Rickenbacker, an American fighter ace in World War I and a Medal of Honor recipient, 1890-1973.

"Bravery is the capacity to perform properly even when scared half to death."
Omar N. Bradley, a senior officer of the United States Army during and after World War II, 1893-1981.

"Courage is fear holding on a minute longer."
George S. Patton, general in the United States Army, 1885-1945.

"The greatest mistake you can make in life is continually fearing that you'll make one."

Elbert Hubbard, American writer, publisher, artist, and philosopher, 1856-1915.

Gaining strength, confidence, and power by doing what you fear

"If it scares you, it might be a good thing to try."
Seth Godin, American author of 17 business success books.

"To uncover your true potential, you must first find your own limits and then you have to have the courage to blow past them."
Picabo Street, an American former World Cup alpine ski racer and Olympic gold medalist.

"We gain strength, and courage, and confidence by each experience in which we really stop to look fear in the face... we must do that which we think we cannot."
Eleanor Roosevelt, former First Lady of the United States, American political figure, diplomat, and activist, 1884-1962.

Living a more fulfilling life

"Life shrinks or expands in proportion to one's courage."
Anais Nin, French-American diarist, essayist, and novelist, 1903-1977.

"What would life be if we had no courage to attempt anything?"
Vincent Van Gogh, Dutch Post-Impressionist painter, known for "The Starry Night," 1853-1890.

"I need to put myself out in the world and be brave and be uncomfortable. When I do, it means I can enjoy life so much more."
Annabelle Wallis, an English actress, known for playing Jane Seymour in Showtime's period drama *The Tudors* from 2009 to 2010.

"It takes courage to grow up and become who you really are."
e.e. Cummings, a poet, painter, essayist, author, and playwright, who wrote approximately 2900 poems, 1894-1962.

"If you are lucky enough to find a way of life you love, you have to find the courage to live it."
John Irving, American novelist and screenwriter.

Understanding, assessing, controlling, and managing your fear

"Courage is not the absence of fear, but rather the assessment that something else is more important than fear."
Franklin D. Roosevelt, 32nd President of the United States, American statesman, and political leader, 1882-1945.

"Courage is a special kind of knowledge: the knowledge of how to fear what ought to be feared and how not to fear what ought not to be feared."
David Ben-Gurion, the primary founder of the State of Israel and its first Prime Minister, 1886-1973.

"Courage is knowing what not to fear."
Plato, a philosopher in Classical Greece and the founder of the Academy in Athens, the first institution of higher learning in the Western world, 428–348 BC.

"Bravery does not mean being fearless. It means to be full of fear but still not being dominated by it."
Rajneesh, Indian mystic and leader of the Rajneesh movement, 1931-1990.

Inspiring others

"Keep your fears to yourself, but share your courage with others."
Robert Louis Stevenson, Scottish novelist, poet, essayist, musician, and travel writer. Author of *Treasure Island* and *The Strange Case of Dr. Jekyll and Mr. Hyde*, 1850-1894.

"Courage is contagious. When a brave man takes a stand, the spines of others are often stiffened."
Billy Graham, American evangelist and ordained Southern Baptist minister, 1918-2018.

FACING FAILURE

The possibility of failure often inspires fear, because success is so highly valued in modern society. Thus, a great many people fear they will fail at something, so they don't try to do it and do something else they value less where success seems more certain. Or people who experience failure don't try to push through it to learn and grow from their failure. By contrast, those who courageously face down failure and act anyway in order to put a failure behind them often succeed.

Examples of pushing through this fear of failure abound in the many success stories of celebrities, business executives, and entrepreneurs. Many pick themselves up multiple times and push on, unafraid to let a failure hold them back.

Following are some quotes from individuals talking about this close relationship of courage and facing down failure to achieve success.

Continuing on despite a failure

"Success is not final, failure is not fatal: it is the courage to continue that counts."
Winston Churchill, British Prime Minister, politician, and army officer, 1874-1965.

"Failure is unimportant. It takes courage to make a fool of yourself."
Charlie Chaplin, English comic actor, filmmaker, and composer, 1889-1977

"Take chances, make mistakes. That's how you grow. Pain nourishes your courage. You have to fail in order to practice being brave."
Mary Tyler Moore, American actress, 1936-2017.

<u>Overcoming the fear of failure and moving on</u>

"Come to the edge.' 'We can't. We're afraid.' 'Come to the edge.' 'We can't. We will fall!' 'Come to the edge.' And they came. And he pushed them. And they flew."
Guillaume Apollinaire, French poet, playwright, short story writer, novelist, and art critic, 1880-1918

"In order to achieve anything you must be brave enough to fail."
Kirk Douglas, American actor, producer, director, and author.

TAKING ON CHALLENGES AND RISKS

Courage also plays a role in striving to overcome challenges and taking risks as necessary to achieve a goal. This attitude can be found in all walks of life, from those who are courageous during a war to those who push through fear to face challenges that scare them in sports, business, and other areas of life.

In many cases, these challenges take the form of obstacles and difficulties to be overcome. But those with courage press on, putting aside their fear to prevail. Even so, taking risks doesn't mean subjecting oneself to unnecessary dangers, since courage is often inspired by wisdom.

Following are some quotes from individuals talking about this close relationship of courage to taking on challenges or making risky choices about what to do.

Facing challenges

"You'll never do a whole lot unless you're brave enough to try."
Dolly Parton, American singer, songwriter, multi-instrumentalist, and record producer.

"Courage is grace under pressure."
Ernest Hemingway, American novelist, short story writer, and journalist, widely acclaimed for *The Old Man and the Sea,* 1899-1961.

"Courage is not simply one of the virtues, but the form of every virtue at the testing point."
C. S. Lewis, British novelist, poet, critic, essayist, and lecturer, 1898-1963.

Overcoming adversity and difficulties

"We don't develop courage by being happy every day. We develop it by surviving difficult times and challenging adversity."
Barbara De Angelis, American relationship consultant, lecturer, and author.

"You must learn to be strong in the dark as well as in the day, else you will always be only half brave."
George MacDonald, Scottish author, poet, and Christian minister, 1824-1905.

"Do not pray for an easy life, pray for the strength to endure a difficult one"
Bruce Lee, Hong Kong and American actor, film director, martial artist, and founder of Jeet Kune Do, 1940-1973.

"Great crisis produce great men and great deeds of courage."
John F Kennedy, an American politician and 35th President of the United States from 1961 until he was assassinated in November 1963, 1917-1963.

Confronting danger

"The bravest are surely those who have the clearest vision of what is before them, glory and danger alike, and yet notwithstanding go out to meet it."
Thucydides, Athenian historian and general, 460–395 BC.

"Courage - a perfect sensibility of the measure of danger, and a mental willingness to endure it."
William Tecumseh Sherman, American soldier, businessman, educator, and author; general in the Union Army during the American Civil War, 1820-1891.

"Courage consists not in blindly overlooking danger, but in seeing it, and conquering it."
Jean Paul, German Romantic writer, 1763-1825.

"Being brave means to know something is scary, difficult, and dangerous, and doing it anyway, because the possibility of winning the fight is worth the chance of losing it."

Emilie Autumn, American singer-songwriter, poet, violinist, and actress.

"Fear can keep a man out of danger but courage only can support him in it."
Thomas Fuller, an English churchman and historian, now remembered for his writings, particularly *Worthies of England*, published in 1662, 1608-1661.

Taking risks in everyday life

"He who is not courageous enough to take risks will accomplish nothing in life."
Muhammad Ali, American professional boxer, activist, and philanthropist, 1942-2016.

"Courage is a love affair with the unknown."
Bhagwan Shree Rajneesh (AKA: Acharya Rajneesh), an Indian godman and leader of the Rajneesh movement, viewed as a controversial new religious movement leader and mystic, 1931-1990.

"And the trouble is, if you don't risk anything, you risk even more."
Erica Jong, American novelist, satirist, and poet; author of the novel *Fear of Flying*.

Taking changes and embracing the unknown

"All growth is a leap in the dark, a spontaneous unpremeditated act without benefit of experience."
Henry Miller, American writer expatriated in Paris, 1891-1980.

"Only those who will risk going too far can possibly find out how far one can go."
T. S. Eliot, American essayist, publisher, playwright, and critic, 1888-1965.

"Who dares nothing, need hope for nothing."
Friedrich Schiller, German poet, philosopher, physician, historian, and playwright, 1759-1805.

"To dare is to lose one's footing momentarily. To not dare is to lose oneself."
Soren Kierkegaard, a Danish philosopher, theologian, poet, social critic and religious author , considered the first existentialist philosopher, 1813-1855.

"You cannot swim for new horizons until you have courage to lose sight of the shore."
William Faulkner, an American writer and Nobel Prize laureate from Mississippi, who wrote novels, short stories, a play, poetry, essays, and screenplays, 1897-1962.

"You can't test courage cautiously."
Annie Dillard, American author of both fiction and non-fiction, who published poetry, essays, prose, and literary criticism, as well as two novels and one memoir.

Being both courageous and wise

"True courage is a result of reasoning. A brave mind is always impregnable.
Jeremy Collier, an English theatre critic, bishop, and theologian, 1650-1726.

"The real man smiles in trouble, gathers strength from distress, and grows brave by reflection."
Thomas Paine, English-American political activist, philosopher, and political theorist, 1737-1809.

"Without courage, wisdom bears no fruit."
Baltasar Gracian, a Spanish Jesuit, baroque prose writer, philosopher, 1601-1658

ACCOMPLISHING GOALS AND ACHIEVING SUCCESS

Courage can be a means to ultimate success, too. Along the way, one may face fears, move through one's comfort zone, and press onward to achieve one's goals. Since overcoming fear or doing what feels uncomfortable can lead to gaining success, individuals are encouraged to take action, despite any fears or discomfort, although one should act reasonably and responsibly.

Following are some quotes from individuals talking about this close relationship of courage to achievement and success.

"All our dreams can come true, if we have the courage to pursue them."
Walt Disney, American entrepreneur, animator, voice actor, and film producer, 1901-1966.

"If you could get up the courage to begin, you have the courage to succeed."
David Viscott, American psychiatrist, author, businessman, and media personality, 1938-1966.

"The key to success is for you to make a habit throughout your life of doing the things you fear."
Brian Tracy, Canadian-American motivational public speaker and self-development author.

"Fortune and love favor the brave."
Ovid, ancient Roman poet. 43 BC-17 AD.

"Whenever you see a successful business, someone once made a courageous decision."

Peter Drucker, Austrian-American management consultant, educator, and author, 1909-2005.

"You will never do anything in this world without courage. It is the greatest quality of the mind next to honor."
Aristotle, ancient Greek philosopher, 384–322 BC.

HAVING FAITH

Being courageous is often connected to faith. Such faith in oneself or a higher being can give one the confidence and assurance to take a risk or move out of one's comfort zone. Having faith can also help one keep going by believing one will ultimately prevail, so one will take that "leap of faith," even when not knowing the outcome.

Often this faith is in a higher power, though it can be a belief in oneself. Then, too, being brave and courageous is sometimes associated with an individual's spiritual essence or soul.

Following are some quotes from individuals talking about this close relationship of courage and faith.

"Courage is fear that has said its prayers."
Dorothy Bernard, American actress of the silent era, 1890-1955.

"Faith is taking the first step even when you don't see the whole staircase."
Martin Luther King, Jr., American Baptist minister and activist for the Civil Rights Movement, 1929-1968.

"Bravery is believing in yourself, and that thing nobody can teach you."
El Cordobes (AKA Manuel Benítez Pérez) a famous matador of the 1960s who brought an acrobatic and theatrical style to the bullring.

"Bravery is not a quality of the body. It is of the soul."
Mahatma Gandhi, an Indian activist who led the Indian independence movement against British rule, 1869-1948.

FREEDOM, INDEPENDENCE, AND CREATIVITY

Courage is additionally associated with being free, independent, and creative, which are all related. For example, creativity is nourished by feeling free to express ones ideas and taking independent action to express them. By being courageous, you are unafraid to say what you think and come up with ideas to create something new. Courage can also involve moving ahead to do something you believe in without needing input or encouragement from others. It can even involve taking some action, when others criticize you or say what you are doing is wrong.

Following are some quotes from individuals talking about this close relationship of courage with freedom, independence, and creativity.

Feeling a sense of freedom

"He who is brave is free."
Lucius Annaeus Seneca, a Roman Stoic philosopher, statesman, and dramatist, 4 BC–65 AD.

Acting and persevering without others support or regardless of what others say

"True bravery is shown by performing without witness what one might be capable of doing before all the world."
Francois de la Rochefoucauld, a noted French author of maxims and memoirs, 1613-1680.

"Whatever you do, you need courage. Whatever course you decide upon, there is always someone to tell you that you are wrong."
Ralph Waldo Emerson, American essayist, lecturer, philosopher, and poet, 1803-1882.

Being creative

"Creativity takes courage."
Henri Matisse, a French Impressionist artist, known for his use of color and fluid use of line, 1869-1954.

"Be brave enough to live life creatively. The creative is the place where no one else has ever been."
Alan Alda, American actor, director, comedian, and screenwriter.

OTHER QUALITIES OF COURAGE

Courage can take many other forms.

It can involve not only taking action, but being willing to listen. One can even take small steps of action, but as long as one takes some action, that shows courage.

Then, too, the more one acts courageously, the more it becomes a habit and is strengthened each time it is expressed. Ironically, many people don't realize they are being courageous, when they are doing something that takes courage.

Often courage can result from caring for or being concerned about others, such as when a parent acts courageously to protect a child.

Some view it as a moral virtue or the foundation for all other virtues.

However, one can avoid having to be courageous, if one is safely away from any challenging situation or danger, or if one lives a protected, cloistered life.

Finally, courage is associated with living life fully and having a happy life, whereas not being courageous can stifle happiness and joy.

Following are some quotes from individuals talking about these different qualities of courage.

Being responsive to others

"Courage is what it takes to stand up and speak; courage is also what it takes to sit down and listen."
Winston Churchill, British Prime Minister, politician, and army officer, 1874-1965.

Not recognizing courage

"What may look like a small act of courage is courage nevertheless. The important thing is to be willing to take a step forward."
Daisaku Ikeda, Japanese Buddhist philosopher, educator, author, and nuclear disarmament advocate.

"Most of us have far more courage than we ever dreamed we possessed."
Dale Carnegie, American writer and lecturer, 1888-1955.

"A hero is no braver than an ordinary man, but he is brave five minutes longer."
Ralph Waldo Emerson, American essayist, lecturer, philosopher, and poet, 1803-1882.

Growing more courageous by acting courageously

"Courage is very important. Like a muscle, it is strengthened by use."
Ruth Gordon, American film, stage, and television actress, 1896-1985.

"Moral excellence comes about as a result of habit. We become just by doing just acts, temperate by doing temperate acts, brave by doing brave acts."
Aristotle, an ancient Greek philosopher, considered, along with Plato, to be the "Father of Western Philosophy," 384– 322 BC.

Acting courageously out of concern for others

"From caring comes courage."
Lao Tzu, an ancient Chinese philosopher, writer, and founder of philosophical Taoism, who reputedly wrote the Tao Te Ching, , born around the 6th century to 533 BC.

Courage as the foundation of other virtues

"Courage is the first of human qualities because it is the quality which guarantees the others."
 Aristotle, ancient Greek philosopher, 384– 322 BC.

"Courage is the greatest of all virtues, because if you haven't courage, you may not have an opportunity to use any of the others."
Samuel Johnson, English writer, poet, essayist, critic, and editor, 1709-1784.

Being courageous to live life fully

"Courage is almost a contradiction in terms. It means a strong desire to live taking the form of readiness to die."
Gilbert K. Chesterton, English writer, poet, philosopher, dramatist, journalist, orator, and lay theologian, 1874-1936.

"Cowards die many deaths before their deaths, the valiant never taste of death but once."
William Shakespeare, an English poet, playwright and actor, widely regarded as the world's pre-eminent dramatist, 1564-1616.

"Happiness is a form of courage."
Holbrook Jackson, British journalist, writer, and publisher, 1874-1948.

Not having a need to show courage

"It is easy to be brave from a safe distance."
Aesop, a Greek storyteller credited with a number of fables, now collectively known as Aesop's Fables, 620–564 BC.

"You can't be brave if you've only had wonderful things happen to you." Mary Tyler Moore, an American actress, known for her roles in television sitcoms, including *The Mary Tyler Moore Show* from 1970 to 1977, 1936-2017.

APPLYING THE PRINCIPLE OF COURAGE IN YOUR LIFE

As the previous sections have described, having courage can contribute to your achieving more success, happiness, and satisfaction in life. Like other qualities, such as forgiveness and gratitude, it can contribute to better relationships with others and bring you more peace and contentment. Importantly, having courage can help you overcome your fears, put failures behind you, and move on to bigger and better things.

Here are some things you can do to have more courage:

1) Keep a courage journal or add a section to your journal where you write down what you feel you need courage to do. These could include fears you want to overcome, people you hope to confront about something, or difficult tasks that are a challenge for you. After you make your list, review each item and imagine yourself having the courage to face each one. Or if it's a long list, prioritize what you want to do and tackle one or two items at a time. Imagine you are overcoming any fears and mastering any challenge. See yourself achieving a goal or being praised for your courage and bravery by others. As you imagine these experiences, feel yourself becoming stronger and more powerful, because you had the courage to do whatever you initially felt unsure about doing.

2) Make a list of 5 to 10 ways in which you have shown courage in the past and 5 to 10 things where you can show courage in the future. Notice if there are any patterns on the lists, like certain types of situations where you have shown courage or expect to do so. Then, take some time to experience in your imagination those situations where you have shown courage. Next imagine yourself showing courage in a future situation. Experience a sense of peacefulness, freedom, power, satisfaction or other positive feelings as a result of what you have done or expect to do.

3) Write up your favorite quotes about courage in large print on separate sheets of paper. Post the quotes around your house where you can see them each day.

4) Take a courage walk around your neighborhood or nearby park. Think about all the times you have shown courage and what you need courage for now. Feel a sense of power or freedom as you imagine that each time you have experienced courage in the past or expect to experience it in the future. Try projecting your feelings of exercising courage onto a bird you see nearby. When the bird flies, imagine you are soaring with the feelings of power or freedom that comes from acting courageously.

5) Pair up with a friend or business associate and take 5-10 minutes to talk about how you have been courageous or brave in the past week or what you need courage to deal with. Or form a weekly or monthly courage group of 3-10 people, where you share with one another for about an hour about your experiences of courage for that past week or month.

6) Create a Vision Board or Vision Board Book, in which you gather images of situations in which you have been courageous or need to be in the future and paste them on your board or in your book. Later, hang the Vision Board on a wall in your house or carry your Vision Board Book with you. Then, you can look at these images from time to time to remind yourself to feel the sense of power and freedom that comes from being courageous.

7) Create a list of 5-10 people where you have done something that involves courage and think about what you did. Notice if there are any patterns in the types of situations where you expressed courage, so you can be even more confident in expressing your courage in the future.

8) Do a meditation on courage for 10-15 minutes on your own or with others. During this time, get relaxed, close your eyes, visualize what you have done to be courageous, and feel that sense of power and freedom that comes from acting out of courage.

9) If you experience difficulty in being courageous, take some time to think about the reasons for this. If needed, discuss this difficulty with others who are working on being more courageous. Or remind yourself how your courage has helped you overcome a fear or difficult situation, so you can feel more confident and powerful in what you can do in the future. Also, remind yourself of any successes you experienced after having the courage to do something that initially felt uncomfortable. Reminding yourself of your past successes in exercising courage can help you be more courageous in the future, despite any fears or challenges you may face.

10) Think of situations where you might exercise courage in the future to push pass any limitations or restrictions you feel are holding you back. Then, imagine what you might do in the future and see yourself succeeding in overcoming any limitations or restrictions.

11) Now it's up to you. Think of other ways you might embrace and express courage to gain whatever success you want and to feel more confidence, freedom, and power.

PART IV: FINDING FORGIVENESS FOR OTHERS AND YOURSELF

INTRODUCTION TO PART IV

After you overcome a challenge, you may find that others have made your experience more difficult due to their mistakes, opposition, or being a rival. You may have regrets over things you did, including mistakes you made or people you hurt or left behind along the way. So you may need to forgive others or yourself.

Forgiveness has a long history - as long as humans have made mistakes or engaged in behaviors that have hurt or angered others. It is an important quality to have in order to forget something bad that has happened and move on. And importantly, one needs to forgive oneself to get over regrets for lost opportunities and relationships.

Often forgiveness is related to having love and compassion for others or oneself. It is sometimes considered a quality of strength and power through showing acceptance of others' failings. It is also associated with being able to start again and embark on new beginnings rather than being stuck in the past.

The following quotes show the many different ways that forgiveness is a valuable quality to have, and how we can embrace that quality to bring more happiness and joy into our lives. The quotes are organized by the different aspects of forgiveness, and each quote includes the name of the person first credited with that quote.

FORGIVENESS AND THE DIVINE

Forgiveness is often associated with the divinity, as a kind of divine redemption or acceptance. In this way, an individual is not only granted forgiveness for mistakes or misdeeds by others and oneself, but from a godly being or higher power. Such forgiveness is like being washed in purifying waters, so one feels restored or redeemed of any continued punishment or negative effects for what one has done.

Another comparison is with the power of the confessional in the Catholic faith, where a person confesses their sins. Afterwards, the priest absolves the confessor for owning up to what they have done or asks them to perform certain tasks or rituals, after which the person can consider himself or herself forgiven.

Commonly, believers can feel more confident in themselves despite any mistakes they make along the way by asking their God for forgiveness. Or they may ask for forgiveness if they don't show enough appreciation for what they have in life which they attribute to the favor of God. But by seeking forgiveness, they can feel themselves absolved and therefore feel more supported by God.

Following are some quotes from individuals talking about this close relationship of forgiveness with the divine.

"To err is human; to forgive, divine."
Alexander Pope, 18th-century English poet, 1688 – 1744

"Never forget the three powerful resources you always have available to you: love, prayer, and forgiveness."
H. Jackson Brown, Jr., American author, best known for his inspirational book, *Life's Little Instruction Book*

"All major religious traditions carry basically the same message, that is love, compassion and forgiveness the important thing is they should be part of our daily lives."
Dalai Lama, the title given to spiritual leaders of the followers of Tibetan Buddhism

"Man has two great spiritual needs. One is for forgiveness. The other is for goodness."
Billy Graham, a prominent American evangelist, who was an ordained Southern Baptist minister, 1918 - 2018

"Forgiveness is not a feeling - it's a decision we make because we want to do what's right before God. It's a quality decision that won't be easy and it may take time to get through the process, depending on the severity of the offense."
Joyce Meyer, a Christian author, speaker, and minister

"Thank you, God, for this good life and forgive us if we do not love it enough."
Garrison Keillor, an American author, storyteller, humorist, voice actor, and radio personality, best known for the Minnesota Public Radio show: *A Prairie Home Companion*

FORGIVENESS AND LOVE

Forgiveness is often associated with love. Some writers see the two as always connected, in that you can't really love someone unless you are willing to forgive them for any failings. In fact, you may have to forgive them again and again to show your love.

Such love is the kind of continuing acceptance a parent shows a child. No matter how many mistakes the child makes, the parent is willing to correct, guide, and forgive the child, along with continuing to love.

By the same token, one might learn to recognize both the good and evil in others, regardless of who they are, and this power to forgive also enables one to love.

Following are some quotes from individuals talking about this close relationship of forgiveness and love.

"There is no love without forgiveness, and there is no forgiveness without love."
Bryant H. McGill, American author, poet, speaker, and activist in the field of human potential and human rights

"Love is an act of endless forgiveness, a tender look which becomes a habit.
Peter Ustinov, British actor, writer, filmmaker, dramatist, who has won many awards, including two Academy Awards.

"We must develop and maintain the capacity to forgive. He who is devoid of the power to forgive is devoid of the power to love. There is some good in the worst of us and some evil in the best of us. When we discover this, we are less prone to hate our enemies."

Martin Luther King, Jr., American Baptist minister and leader of the 1960s American civil rights movement, 1929 - 1968

"I believe forgiveness is the best form of love in any relationship. It takes a strong person to say they're sorry and an even stronger person to forgive."

Yolanda Hadid, Dutch-American TV personality and former model, best known as a star of the American reality-TV show *The Real Housewives of Beverly Hills*

FORGIVENESS AND COMPASSION

For some, forgiveness is a way to express compassion. As such, it involves recognizing the hardships and difficulties others have suffered that may have led them to do something wrong for which they need forgiveness. Then, too, by showing compassion for someone, you show you recognize their ability to change and do good, even though they have done wrong in the past.

In this way, compassion shows understanding and empathy for the other person and what they have experienced, and it gives them another chance to change for the better. Such compassion means having a good heart towards others, and it releases one from the burden that comes from being hard-hearted, such as feeling hate, resentfulness, and being stuck in negative emotions from the past. Forgiveness might also be linked with love, in that one may show love towards the person for whom one feels compassion.

Following are some quotes that show that relationship of forgiveness with showing understanding and compassion for others.

"For me, forgiveness and compassion are always linked: how do we hold people accountable for wrongdoing and yet at the same time remain in touch with their humanity enough to believe in their capacity to be transformed?"
Bell Hooks, an American author, feminist, and social activist

"Our lack of forgiveness makes us hate, and our lack of compassion makes us hard-hearted. Pride in our hearts makes us resentful and keeps our memory in a constant whirlwind of passion and self-pity."

Mother Angelica, an Catholic American Franciscan nun, best known for her television personality, as founder of the Eternal Word Television Network, 1923 – 2016

FORGIVENESS AND PEACE

Forgiveness is often thought of as a way to find peace and to calm the mind. Otherwise, one can continue to feel hurt or anger over something that has happened due to the actions of oneself or others. But if one can forgive, that hurt and anger goes away, so one feels peaceful and calm again.

While it can be hard to get over whatever caused that pain, forgiveness is a way to overcome that hurdle. It is a way to confront and overcome any feelings of anger. Additionally, it is a way to smooth over whatever has caused one pain, so one stops dwelling on that pain, which brings one peace.

At the same time, it can be easier to forgive oneself or others when one is already feeling calm and peaceful, or content and satisfied.

Following are some quotes that show that relationship of forgiveness with finding peace and calm in one's life again.

"Forgiveness is not always easy. At times, it feels more painful than the wound we suffered, to forgive the one that inflicted it. And yet, there is no peace without forgiveness."
Marianne Williamson, an American spiritual teacher, author, and lecturer, who has published twelve books, best known for *A Return to Love*

"When a deep injury is done us, we never recover until we forgive."
Alan Paton, a South African author and anti-apartheid activist, best known for the novel *Cry, the Beloved Country.* 1903 – 1988

"Confront the dark parts of yourself, and work to banish them with illumination and forgiveness. Your willingness to wrestle with your demons will cause your angels to sing."
August Wilson, an American playwright whose work included the series, *The Pittsburgh Cycle*, for which he received two Pulitzer Prizes for drama, 1945 – 2005

"Genuine forgiveness does not deny anger but faces it head-on."
Alice Miller, Swiss psychologist, psychoanalyst, and philosopher, best known for her books on parental child abuse, 1923-2010.

"One of the secrets of a long and fruitful life is to forgive everybody everything every night before you go to bed."
Bernard Baruch, American businessman, who served as an economic advisor to Presidents Woodrow Wilson and Franklin D. Roosevelt.

"When I am able to resist the temptation to judge others, I can see them as teachers of forgiveness in my life, reminding me that I can only have peace of mind when I forgive rather than judge. "
Dr. Gerald Jampolsky, American physician and author on psychiatry, health, business, and education. Well-known for his book *Love is Letting go of Fear.*

"When you are happy you can forgive a great deal."
Princess Diana, the first wife of Charles, Prince of Wales, and the mother of Prince William, Duke of Cambridge, and Prince Harry, Duke of Sussex, 1901-1997.

FORGIVENESS, STRENGTH, AND COURAGE

Some may think that forgiveness is a sign of weakness, in that the person who is forgiving is giving in. They appear to be accepting whatever wrong the other person has done to them or whatever mistakes he or she has made.

But this characterization of forgiveness is not true. Rather, the person who forgives commonly receives praise for their strength and courage. They are depicted as being fearless and powerful in their willingness to forgive the trespass of others, as it says in the Bible. They are able to reaffirm a relationship by the act of forgiveness, which may gain them the support, trust, and loyalty of the person they have forgiven.

Again and again, the person who forgives is praised for being strong and brave for their act of forgiving others, including their enemies. So like trust, forgiveness helps solidify the bonds of relationships in society by showing that the person who has committed wrongful actions can be redeemed. Moreover, showing this person renewed faith and support for the future is a sign of strength, not weakness.

Following are some quotes that show that relationship of forgiveness with showing understanding and compassion for others.

"The weak can never forgive. Forgiveness is the attribute of the strong."
Mahatma Gandhi, Indian activist and leader of the Indian independence movement against British rule, 1869 - 1948

"Forgiveness is a virtue of the brave.
Indira Gandhi, first and only female Prime Minister of India, before her assassination in 1984, 1917 - 1984

"Only the brave know how to forgive... a coward never forgave; it is not in his nature.
Laurence Sterne, Irish-born English novelist, Anglican clergyman, and author of the novel *The Life and Opinions of Tristram Shandy*, 1713 - 1768

"We think that forgiveness is weakness, but it's absolutely not; it takes a very strong person to forgive."
T. D. Jakes, American pastor, author, and filmmaker; most known for founding the Potter's House, a non-denominational American mega-church

FORGIVENESS AND LETTING GO, MOVING ON, AND NEW BEGINNINGS

Forgiving is commonly viewed as a way of healing from whatever has happened in order to let go, move on, and begin again. Doing so becomes freeing. It's a way to leave behind the past and feel a sense of freedom, sometimes by forgetting what happened.

Forgiving also enables one to feel release from feelings of anger, resentment, and hurt from whatever injury occurred, so one can recover. It is a source of mending and healing through letting go and moving forward. It is a way of moving towards a better future. Otherwise, without forgiving, one can get stuck in anger, resentment, and seeking revenge, making it difficult if not impossible to move on.

Following are some quotes that show these themes.

"Forgiveness says you are given another chance to make a new beginning."
Desmond Tutu, South African Anglican cleric and theologian, known for his work as an anti-apartheid and human rights activist

"To forgive is to set a prisoner free and discover that the prisoner was you."
Lewis B. Smedes, a renowned Christian author, ethicist, and theologian, whose 15 books include *Forgive and Forget: Healing the Hurts We Don't Deserve*, 1921-2002

"The most important thing that I learned in growing up is that forgiveness is something that, when you do it, you free yourself to move on."
Tyler Perry, an American director, screenwriter, actor, and comedian

"When you forgive, you in no way change the past - but you sure do change the

future."
Bernard Meltzer, nationally syndicated radio host, known for his advice call-in show, *What's Your Problem?* 1916 – 1998

"Holding on to anger, resentment and hurt only gives you tense muscles, a headache and a sore jaw from clenching your teeth. Forgiveness gives you back the laughter and the lightness in your life."
Joan Lunden, American journalist, author, and a television host on ABC's *Good Morning America* from 1980 to 1997

"Forgiveness means letting go of the past."
Dr. Gerald Jampolsky, American physician and author on psychiatry, health, business, and education. Well-known for his book *Love is Letting go of Fear.*

"Forgiveness is the key to action and freedom."
Hannah Arendt, a German-born American philosopher, political theorist, and author on topics ranging from totalitarianism to epistemology, 1906 - 1975

"Forgiveness is a way of opening up the doors again and moving forward, whether it's a personal life or a national life."
Hillary Clinton, American politician, who was First Lady of the U.S. from 1993 to 2001 and U.S. Secretary of State from 2009 to 2014

"The remedy for life's broken pieces is not classes, workshops or books. Don't try to heal the broken pieces. Just forgive."
Iyanla Vanzant, American inspirational speaker, author, life coach, lawyer, and spiritual teacher

"Forgiveness is the needle that knows how to mend."
Jewel Kilcher, American singer-songwriter, musician, producer, actress, author, poet, and four-time Grammy award nominee

"Without forgiveness life is governed by... an endless cycle of resentment and retaliation."
Roberto Assagioli, Italian psychiatrist, pioneer of humanistic and transpersonal psychology, and founder of the psychosynthesis movement, 1888-1974

FORGIVENESS, MAKING MISTAKES, AND ACCEPTANCE

Forgiving also means acknowledging one's mistakes or those of others, accepting them, and moving past them. In doing so, one might learn from such mistakes for the future or recognize that we all make errors, since to err is part of being human, because no one is perfect.

Likewise, forgiving can mean accepting certain qualities that are part of someone's personality, so he or she can't change. However, sometimes a person may have certain characteristics that can't be accepted and therefore forgiven, such if he or she is continually and intentionally cruel or is an evil, destructive person who wants to be released from blame, only to act cruelly again. But otherwise, a person with certain personal qualities, such as being selfish and egotistic, can be forgiven for being who he or she is.

Then, too, forgiving can involve recognizing that one lacks certain knowledge, so that one needs to be open and accepting, which can include forgiving oneself and others.

Following are some quotes that reflect these themes.

"Mistakes are always forgivable, if one has the courage to admit them."
Bruce Lee, martial-arts legend, 1940 - 1973

"The lesson is that you can still make mistakes and be forgiven."
Robert Downey, Jr., American actor, well-known for his roles as Iron Man in the Marvel Cinematic Universe and in the *Avenger* series.

"Selfishness must always be forgiven you know, because there is no hope of a cure."
Jane Austen, an English novelist known primarily for her six major novels about the British landed gentry at the end of the 18th century, 1775 – 1817

"Just knowing you don't have the answers is a recipe for humility, openness, acceptance, forgiveness, and an eagerness to learn - and those are all good things."
Dick Van Dyke, American actor, comedian, writer, singer, dancer, producer, and host of the Dick Van Dyke Show

"Forgive yourself for your faults and your mistakes and move on."
Les Brown, An American motivational speaker, author, radio DJ, and former television host

FORGIVENESS AND FORGETTING

Forgiveness is closely associated with forgetting, since forgetting can enable one to let go of what happened in the past. The memory might still be there, but the goal of forgetting is to not dwell on bad feelings and regrets for what occurred, but to no longer remember and let go of such feelings. It is like closing a chapter in a book, moving on to the next, and forgetting what is unimportant in the past.

This notion of forgetting to forgive is expressed in various ways, such as burying the hatchet, tearing up a note, and not being trapped by past hardships or past iterations of the self. In this way, through forgetting, one can become something new, like a phoenix rising from the ashes. The phoenix is the new rejuvenated creature, while the ashes represent what one wishes to forget.

Often it can be hard to forget, but it is a necessary part of forgiveness - this cancellation of something that went wrong in the past.

Following are some quotes that show these themes.

"You build on failure. You use it as a stepping stone. Close the door on the past. You don't try to forget the mistakes, but you don't dwell on it. You don't let it have any of your energy, or any of your time, or any of your space."
Johnny Cash, American singer-songwriter and country music icon, 1932-2003

"The only thing I've settled in my mind is that I want to forgive, and forgiveness comes with forgetting."
Ingrid Betancourt, Colombian-French politician, former senator, and anti-corruption activist

"I took revenge on hardship from my earlier life by forgetting it."
Alija Izetbegovic, Bosnian politician and activist. first president of the Republic of Bosnia and Herzegovina from 1992-2000, 1925-2003.

"If you will work in co-operation, forgetting the past, burying the hatchet, you are bound to succeed."
Muhammad Ali Jinnah, founder and Pakistan's first Governor General of Pakistan, 1876-1948.

"

Our sense of worth, of well-being, even our sanity depends upon our remembering. But, alas, our sense of worth, our well-being, our sanity also depends upon our forgetting.
Joyce Appleby, American historian, 1929-2016.

"I can forgive, but I cannot forget, is only another way of saying, I will not forgive. Forgiveness ought to be like a cancelled note - torn in two, and burned up, so that it never can be shown against one."
Henry Ward Beecher, American clergyman and social reformer, known for supporting the abolition of slavery, 1813-1887.

THE IMPORTANCE OF FORGIVING OTHERS

Forgiving others also contributes to better relationships with them. Through forgiveness, others can work together better as a team, much as trust helps to bind people together, because they feel they can count on others for mutual support. That's because if a team member makes a mistake or does something to damage the relationship with others in the group, forgiveness enables the group to come back together, since the wrong has been forgiven.

In some cases, it can take time for healing to take place, since others may question a person's sincerity in seeking forgiveness or may want the person to show some remorse or repentance for that forgiveness to be granted. Then, too, if one repeatedly makes mistakes or acts in bad faith, it may be harder to forgive that person -- and that person may not merit forgiveness for a long time if forever. But with those qualifications, in general, forgiveness is valued for helping and healing relationships.

This spirit of forgiveness might even provide the basis for world healing, though this may seem an impossible goal. Yet again and again, there are examples of countries forgiving acts of hostility and war to become friends and work together. One key to this ability to move on together is the ability to forgive the past.

The following quotes express these themes.

"It's one of the greatest gifts you can give yourself, to forgive. Forgive everybody."
Maya Angelou, an American poet, singer, memoirist, and civil rights activist, 1928 – 2014

"Forgive me my nonsense, as I also forgive the nonsense of those that think they talk sense."
Robert Frost, an American poet who won four Pulitzer prizes, 1874 – 1963

"I invite everyone to choose forgiveness rather than division, teamwork over personal ambition."
Jean-Francois Cope, French politician and mayor of Meaux

"It's toughest to forgive ourselves. So it's probably best to start with other people. It's almost like peeling an onion. Layer by layer, forgiving others, you really do get to the point where you can forgive yourself."
Patty Duke, American actress, most well-known for her role as Helen Keller in *The Miracle Worker*.

"You will know that forgiveness has begun when you recall those who hurt you and feel the power to wish them well."
Lewis B. Smedes, American theologian. Author of *Forgive and Forget: Healing the Hurts we Don't Deserve, 1921-2002*

"Forgive, forget. Bear with the faults of others as you would have them bear with yours."
Phillips Brooks, an American Episcopal clergyman, author, long the rector of Boston's Trinity Church, 1835 – 1893

"Life is life. You have to learn how to forgive people and how to gain forgiveness for yourself."
Benjamin Clementine, British singer-songwriter

"I think we learn the most from imperfect relationships - things like forgiveness and compassion.
Andrea Thompson, American actress, known for her roles on the TV series *Falcon Crest* and *NYPD Blue*

"The practice of forgiveness is our most important contribution to the healing of the world."
Marianne Williamson, American spiritual teacher, author, and lecturer, who has published twelve books, best known for *A Return to Love*
.

FORGIVING ENEMIES

One of the ironies in thinking about forgiveness is what to do about one's enemies. Should one forgive them?

In general, the answer is "yes," although you might hold back from fully granting that acceptance by conditionally offering your forgiveness, yet remembering what they have done. This way you may be more cautious in dealing with them in the future, in case they wrong you again. If they do, remembering can help you decide what to do, which may include withdrawing your forgiveness.

Another irony is that forgiveness can sometimes serve as a kind of revenge against your enemies or others who have wronged you, perhaps due to anger towards you. But when you forgive, you diffuse that anger, which could help to heal a fractured relationship. Or perhaps your forgiveness may annoy someone who is angry, because it makes it difficult for them to continue to be hostile to you.

Finally, still another irony is that it may be easier to forgive an enemy than a friend, because the enemy has behaved in expected ways. Therefore, it is simpler to let go of that anger, like turning off a water faucet so the water stops. But a relationship with a friend can be more complex, so if a friend does something hurtful, you might feel a mix of emotions, including feeling betrayed that the friend has broken your bonds of trust. Moreover, if the relationship is a long-term one, it could be full of many complications, twists and turns in feelings for that person. Thus, forgiving may be more difficult, because the emotions surrounding what happened are more complex.

The following quotes express these themes

"Forgive your enemies, but never forget their names."
John F. Kennedy, the 35th U.S. President from January 1961 until his November 1963 assassination, 1917 - 1963

"There is no revenge so complete as forgiveness."
Josh Billings, the pen name of the famous American humor writer and lecturer Henry Wheeler Shaw, 1818 – 1885

"Always forgive your enemies - nothing annoys them so much."
Oscar Wilde, a popular Irish poet and playwright, best remembered for his epigrams, plays, and novel *The Picture of Dorian Gray*, 1854 – 1900

"It is easier to forgive an enemy than to forgive a friend."
William Blake, an English poet, painter, and printmaker, 1757 - 1827

THE DIFFICULTY OF FORGIVENESS

Despite all the benefits of forgiveness, it still can be very difficult to truly forgive. One may remain caught up in the negative feelings about what happened. For example, one can continue to feel anger at a betrayal; one can regret a mistake that led to a loss; one can continue to distrust someone who has engaged in harmful acts. Or some people may resist forgiving since they see it as a weakness rather than a strength. Thus, there can be many reasons why one doesn't want to grant forgiveness to someone or to oneself.

Yet, regardless of the reasons, one needs to recognize these difficulties and work on overcoming them in order to forgive. In fact, sometimes forgiveness requires the will and determination to do this, despite one's feelings of resistance.

The following quotes express this theme.

"Most of us need time to work through pain and loss. We can find all manner of reasons for postponing forgiveness. One of these reasons is waiting for the wrongdoers to repent before we forgive them. Yet such a delay causes us to forfeit the peace and happiness that could be ours."
James E. Faust, an American religious leader, lawyer, and politician, 1920 - 1995

"Forgiveness is hard for me, man. It is for most American-Western males. It's a sign of weakness."
Art Alexakis, American singer-songwriter and guitarist of the rock band Everclear.

"I learned a long time ago that some people would rather die than forgive. It's a strange truth, but forgiveness is a painful and difficult process."
Sue Monk Kidd, American writer. Author of *The Secret Life of Bees*.

"Forgiveness is an act of the will, and the will can function regardless of the temperature of the heart."
Corrie ten Boom, Dutch resistance hero and writer, author of *The Hiding Place*, about her family's efforts to help Jews escape the Nazi Holocaust.

FORGIVENESS AND PERMISSION

Forgiveness is sometimes thought of as a kind of bargaining chip or payment that one might request from another person or even from God if one does something wrong. Then, given this option, one is willing to chance being caught in wrongdoing, since one can always ask for forgiveness and hopefully get it. Or maybe one might imagine engaging in a guilty pleasure and later forgiving oneself.

    Here are some quotes that reflect this theme.

"It is often easier to ask for forgiveness than to ask for permission."
Grace Hopper, American computer scientist and rear admiral in the U.S. Navy, one of the first computer programmers, 1906-1992

"When I was a kid I used to pray every night for a new bicycle. Then I realized that the Lord doesn't work that way so I stole one and asked Him to forgive me."
Emo Philips, American stand-up comedian, voice actor, writer, and producer

APPLYING THE PRINCIPLE OF FORGIVENESS IN YOUR LIFE

As the previous chapters have described, being able to forgive others and yourself can contribute to having a more satisfying and fulfilling life. This forgiveness can contribute to better relationships with others and bring you more peace and contentment. Importantly, forgiving can help you let go of negative emotions, such as anger, resentment, and regret that are holding you back, so you can let go, move on, and feel freer.

Such forgiveness is a principle in all religious traditions, whereby individuals are freed from any sins, transgressions, and past errors through a ritual purification, confession, cleansing, or other method to make the person feel complete and whole again.

When you have a forgiving attitude, this tends to draw others to you, because they feel welcomed and accepted, rather than feeling judged or put down by someone with a negative, critical, judgmental attitude.

In short, as discussed in the introduction to each section and expressed in the quotes, having a forgiving attitude in life offers many benefits.

Here are some things you can do to be more forgiving yourself:

1) Keep a forgiveness journal or add a section to your journal where you write down what you want forgiven or what you are forgiving yourself or others for. Then, review each item on the list, and imagine yourself forgiving that particular item. See it evaporate or crumble in your imagination, and as it does experience yourself letting go and feeling freer and freer, now that you have forgiven yourself or others for that item.

2) Make a list of 10 to 20 things you have forgiven, both of yourself and others. Notice if there are any patterns on the lists, like repeatedly forgiving the same person for something or repeatedly forgiving different people for the same thing. Then, go through another release ritual where you see the things you are forgiving washed away. At the same time, if you notice recurring patterns, ask yourself why, and consider what you might do or change, so those things don't happen so much in the future.

3) Write up your favorite quotes about forgiveness in large print on separate sheets of paper. Then, post the quotes around your house where you can see them each day.

4) Take a forgiveness walk around your neighborhood or nearby park. Think about all the things you have forgiven or what you might need to forgive now. Feel a sense of lightness or freedom as you imagine that each thing you have forgiven is flying away into the trees or bushes you see around you as you walk.

5) Pair up with a friend or business associate and take about 5-10 minutes to talk about what you have forgiven in the past week or what you need to forgive now. Or form a weekly or monthly forgiveness group of 3-10 people, where you share with one another for about 30-60 minutes about your experiences of forgiveness for that week or month.

6) Create a Vision Board or Vision Board Book, in which you gather images of the things you have forgiven or need to forgive and paste them on your board or in your book. Then, hang the board on a wall in your house or carry the book with you, so you can look at these images from time to time to remind yourself to feel this release and freedom that comes from forgiving and letting go.

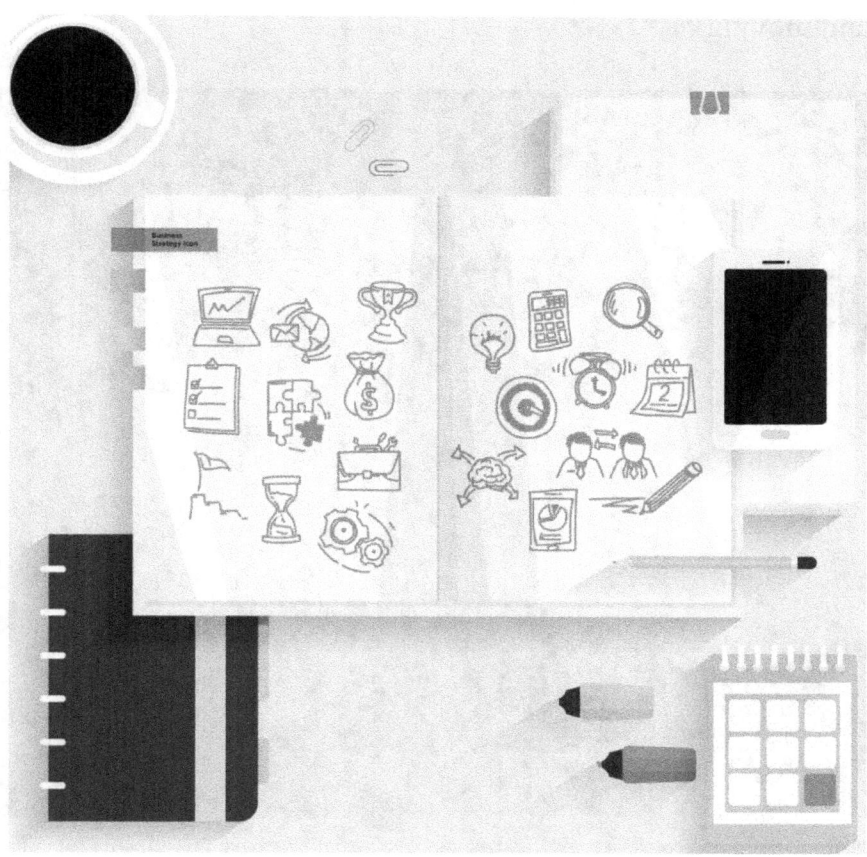

7) Create a list of 5-10 people you have forgiven or need to forgive for something, and think about what they did to need forgiveness. Notice if there are any patterns in one person's behaviors or in the type of things you have had to forgive them for. If so, think of how you might change those behaviors or the types of things you had to forgive, so forgiveness is less necessary.

8) Do a forgiveness meditation for 10-15 minutes on your own or with others. During this time, get relaxed, close your eyes, and while in this calm, meditative state, visualize what you have forgiven and feel that sense of release and freedom that comes from letting go and moving on. Or meditate on what you need to forgive someone or yourself for, and imagine yourself granting that forgiveness. As you do, feel a sense of satisfaction and freedom for granting that forgiveness and letting go of any negative emotions you have held onto because of what happened in the past. If you have any feelings of anger, resentment, hatred, sadness, or other negative emotions, see them flow out of your body and away into the universe, so you feel a sense of renewal and regeneration that comes with letting go and moving on.

9) If you experience difficulty in forgiving and letting go, take some time to think about the reasons you are having difficulty. If needed discuss this difficulty with the person you are having trouble forgiving or with others who may help you forgive. If you talk to the person you find it difficult to forgive, perhaps you might better understand what happened or the person might act to make amends so you can forgive. Or talking to a neutral third party, teacher, priest, counselor, or understanding friend might help you forgive and move on. You might also think about how you have been able to forgive in the past and how that can help you to forgive and let go now. Reminding yourself of your past success in forgiving can help you put aside whatever emotions are holding you back now, while you replace them with a sense of forgiveness and feelings of relaxation, peace, contentment, and freedom that come when you forgive and move on.

10) Think of situations where you might forgive people you haven't forgiven to strengthen or renew those relationships. For example, you might have forgiven someone in your mind but haven't told the person you have done so. You might call or email that person to revive the relationship, and as appropriate, mention the incident that might be a barrier between you and indicate that you don't want what happened in the past to continue to keep you apart. You don't have to say the word "forgiveness," and sometimes it might be better not to say the word, since that might lead the person to think you are blaming that person for being at fault, when he or she feels unfairly judged. So in many cases it can be better to simply say you want to put whatever happened in the past and move on, because you value the person or relationship. In your mind you may feel you are forgiving this person for what he or she has done, but it might be more diplomatic to not put what you are feeling in words that might spark a new conflict.

11) Now it's up to you. Think of other ways you might engage in forgiveness to release and let go of whatever negative feelings you are still holding about something. Just think of all the different ways you might forgive different people or yourself for different situations, and use forgiveness to create more space for peace, harmony, and joy in your life.

PART V: FEELING GRATITUDE

INTRODUCTION TO PART V

After you overcome or finish dealing with a challenge, it can help to feel gratitude for what you have accomplished or learned from the experience. This way you can feel a sense of completion and satisfaction that provides a closure. Such gratitude can be expressed to others, who will appreciate the sentiment, and to yourself, where you think about and feel grateful for what you experienced or what you have now. Then, too, by reflecting about what you feel grateful for, you can better deal with disappointments and difficulties that occur at work and in your personal life.

Likewise, at a time when the world has been confronted by serious challenges due to economic and social upheavals, it's more important than ever to overcome any feelings of gloom and doom and stay positive and upbeat. Expressing gratitude is one way. It's a reminder to think about all the advantages you have. so you can better accept the way things are now. Then, you can feel better and be more hopeful about the future. It's the philosophy of "it is what it is," but express that sentiment in an appreciative way, not with a defeatist attitude that suggests you are resigned to how it's will be, because you think change isn't possible.

Feeling gratitude and expressing thanks to others is extremely important both for feeling satisfaction and for having better relationships with others. Feeling this gratitude is based on accepting what is now, when you can't make any changes, so it's best to acknowledge this situation, rather than feeling upset and discouraged. Not only will you feel better, but that attitude will help you keep going, so you can later change the future to a more positive outcome. It's an idea expressed in the well-known serenity quote from Reinhold Niebuhr, the noted American theologian. As he said in a sermon at the Heath Evangelical Union Church in Heath, Massachusetts, in 1934:

> "God, grant me the serenity to accept
> The things I cannot change,
> Courage to change the things I can,
> And wisdom to know the difference.

One reason that this concept of gratitude has become widely embraced now is a reaction to today's tumultuous times and the current political situation. Many people are responding to the real dangers today with fear, and many people are very afraid that their ability to earn a living is on the line. Even so, apart from the previous suggestions on dealing with anger and fear, and feeling courage and forgiveness, gratitude can provide a sense of release and contentment when you are grateful for what you have, in spite of any hardships you may face.

This gratitude can take many forms, from gratitude for one's home and possessions to being grateful for one's skills, job opportunities, business achievements, and relationships. In turn, this positive attitude makes people feel better by focusing on what they have and not on what they lack. Also, it helps people have better relationships by associating with others with a similar positive and self-affirming outlook. Then, too, being grateful inspires people to continue working towards positive changes, since they are not stuck in regretting what happened in the past, so they can work towards a better future.

In short, feeling and expressing gratitude bring many benefits. In that spirit, I have collected quotes by others, many of them well-known, about the importance of gratitude in everyday life. I have grouped them into the different ways that individuals express gratitude or gain benefits from feeling and acting out of gratitutde.

THE VALUE OF GRATITUDE

Feeling gratitude is widely celebrated as an essential value. It is associated with other positive values, such as love, respect, tolerance, and forgiveness. It is associated with providing service, giving to others, and being a good, righteous person.

Being grateful is also viewed as a way to experience fulfillment in everyday life by turning routine activities into a positive satisfying experience or even a blessing. Then, too, having gratitude shifts one's attention from what one lacks to appreciating what one has, and it improves one's relationships and health. It makes life more fulfilling, and it changes negatives, such as problems, failures, and mistakes, into opportunities for learning and success. It can replace fear, too, so one is better able to move forward to achieve one's goals.

The following quotes express these themes.

"Gratitude is not only the greatest of virtues, but the parent of all others."

Marcus Tutlius Cicero , a Roman philosopher, politician, lawyer, orator, political theorist, consul, and constitutionalist, 106 BC-43 BC

"The greatest wisdom is in simplicity. Love, respect, tolerance, sharing, gratitude, forgiveness…The real knowledge is free…All you need is within you. Great teachers have said that from the beginning. Find your heart, and you will find your way."

Carlos Barrios, Mayan elder and ceremonial priest and spiritual guide of the Eagle Clan

"When we replace a sense of service and gratitude with a sense of entitlement and expectation, we quickly see the demise of our relationships, society, and economy."

Steve Maraboli, Author of *Unapologetically You: Reflections on Life and the Human Experience*

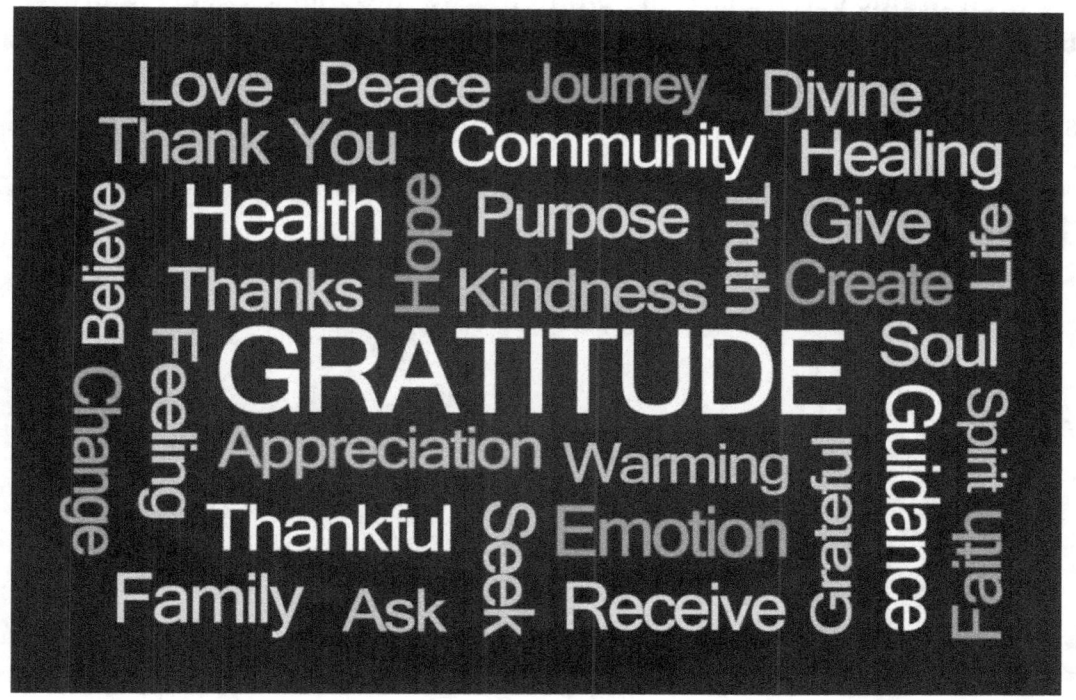

"Gratitude is one of the virtues of the noble man. It is the hallmark of a life lived well. It is a trademark of the righteous man. It is an attribute that significantly impacts on your personal happiness and how sound your relationship will be with others."
Sesan Kareem, speaker, pharmacist, life coach and author of books on self-development

"Gratitude can transform common days into thanksgivings, turn routine jobs into joy, and change ordinary opportunities into blessings."
William Arthur Ward, motivational speaker and author of many inspirational quotes, 1921-1994

"Gratitude is a vaccine, an antitoxin, and an antiseptic."
John Henry Jowett, British Protestant Preacher, known as "The greatest preacher in the English-speaking world"

"Gratitude shifts your focus from what your life lacks to the abundance that is already present. In addition, behavioral and psychological research has shown that giving thanks makes people more resilient, it strengthens relationships, it improves health, and it reduces stress. Gratitude will change your life for the better."
Marelisa Fabrega, lawyer, entrepreneur and owner of daringtolivefully.com

"Gratitude unlocks the fullness of life. It turns what we have into enough, and more. It turns denial into acceptance, chaos into order, confusion into clarity…It turns problems into gifts, failures into success, the unexpected into perfect timing, and mistakes into important events. Gratitude makes sense of our past, brings peace for today and creates a vision for tomorrow.

Melody Beattie, American author of self-help books on codependent relationships

"Replace fear with gratitude, and the whole world changes."
Terri Guillemets, quotation anthologist and author of *A Renewed Outlook, 2007*

"Gratitude is the music of the heart, when its chords are swept by the breeze of kindness.
Author Unknown

EXPRESSING GRATITUDE

If you feel gratitude, express it, too. Don't keep the feeling inside you; instead, share these feelings with others. Let them know you are grateful for something they have done to show your appreciation. Or let them know if you feel grateful generally, as a way to inspire and energize them.

In turn, this expression of gratitude will help you feel more connected to others and them to you. It will help you feel more uplifted and positive.

The following quotes express these ideas.

"Gratitude is the healthiest of all human emotions.... The more you recognize and express gratitude for the things you have, the more things you will have to express gratitude for."

Hilary Hinton aka "Zig" Ziglar, motivational speaker, salesman and author, *Better than Good: Creating a Life You Can't Wait to Live,* 1926-2012

"Expressing gratitude is a natural state of being and reminds us that we are all connected."

Valerie Elster, energy healer and spiritual teacher

"Feeling gratitude and not expressing it is like wrapping a present and not giving it."

William Arthur Ward, motivational speaker and author of many inspirational quotes, 1921-1994

"We are constituted so that simple acts of kindness, such as giving to charity or expressing gratitude, have a positive effect on our long term moods."

Paul Bloom, Canadian American psychologist and professor at Yale University

"Gratitude is what you feel. Thanksgiving is what you do."

Tim Keller, an American pastor, theologian and author of, *The Reason for God: Belief in an Age of Skepticism*

"Gratitude should not be just a reaction to getting what you want, but an all-the-time gratitude, the kind where you notice the little things and where you constantly look for the good, even in unpleasant situations. Start bringing gratitude to your experiences, instead of waiting for a positive experience in order to feel grateful."
Marelisa Fabrega, lawyer, entrepreneur, and owner of daringtolivefully.com

"I woke up this morning as I do every morning, with an attitude of gratitude."
Tony Williams, author of *Minecraft*

"Embrace every new day with gratitude, hope and love."
Lailah Gifty Akita, a Ghanaian and founder of the Smart Youth Volunteers Foundation, author of *Think Great: Be Great!*

"We often take for granted the very things that most deserve our gratitude."

Cynthia Ozick, an American short story writer novelist, essayist, author of *The Pagan Rabbi and Other Stories*

"Gratitude and attitude are not challenges; they are choices."

Robert Braathe, Founder of Braathe Enterprises, online professor, and former manager at Walt Disney World, Gap and Apple

"When I started counting my blessings, my whole life turned around."

Willie Nelson, American musician, singer, songwriter and author

GRATITUDE ABOUT YOURSELF

Feeling gratitude also includes feeling grateful about who you are. It means accepting yourself for not only your skills and accomplishments but for your faults and flaws. It involves not envying others or experiencing regret for the skills you don't have, because you do not have certain qualities or did not take time to develop them. Finally, this self-gratitutde means accepting any disabilities and being grateful for what you have, so you can make the best life possible from what you have been given.

The following quotes express these ideas.

"Take full account of what Excellencies you possess, and in gratitude remember how you would hanker after them, if you had them not."
Marcus Aurelius, Roman Emperor from 161 to 180 A.D., Author of *Meditations*, 121-180 A.D.

"Often people ask how I manage to be happy despite having no arms and no legs. The quick answer is that I have a choice. I can be angry about not having limbs, or I can be thankful that I have a purpose. I chose gratitude."

Nick Vujicic, Australian Christian Evangelist and motivational speaker born with a rare disorder resulting in the absence of arms and legs

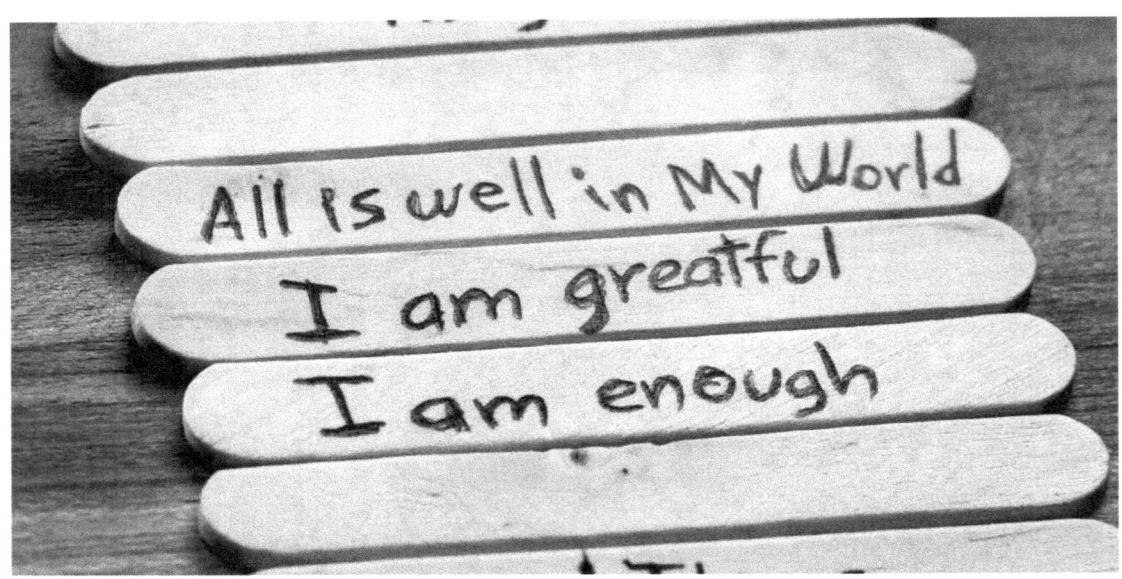

HAPPINESS

A result of feeling grateful for who you are, what you have, and what you experience is that you feel more peaceful and happy. You feel calmer, content and joyous; you experience more pleasure in life. And you go through every day with your heart and soul filled with happiness, because your attitude is one of gratitude.

Researchers have found this to be true – that the people who embrace gratitude are the happiest. They bring this happiness to others, as well, by not only sharing their joy and positive outlook, but by being kind and decent. Being grateful also helps you overcome any feelings of sadness, depression, disappointment, loss, and regret. By being grateful, you focus on what is good in your life and push the bad away or transform it into something positive, so you feel happier.

The following quotes express these ideas.

"Being grateful for what you have is the key to peace and happiness."
Pravin Agarwal, Indian software engineer, author of *8 Course Meal for The Soul*

"Gratitude is a powerful catalyst for happiness. It's the spark that lights a fire of joy in your soul."
Amy Collette, book coach, founder of Unleash Your Inner Author, author of *The Gratitude Connection*

"Happiness is itself a kind of gratitude."
Joseph Wood Krutch, American writer, critic and naturalist, best known for his books on the American Southwest. 1893 –1970

"Gratitude is an overflow of the pleasure of filling your soul."
Raheel Farooq, writer in Punjab, Pakistan, the author of *Zaar*

"Joy is the simplest form of gratitude."
Karl Barth, a Swiss Reformed theologian, 1886 - 1968

"Joy is a heart full and a mind purified by gratitude."
Marietta McCarty, author of *Little Big Minds: Sharing Philosophy with Kids* and Nautilus Award winner for *How Philosophy Can Save Your Life: 10 Ideas That Matter Most*.

"Gratitude helps you to grow and expand; gratitude brings JOY and laughter into your life and into the lives of all those around you."
Eileen Caddy, spiritual teacher, founder of the Findhorn Foundation in Scotland, author of *Opening Doors Within.* 1917 - 2006

"There is a calmness to a life lived in gratitude, a quiet joy."
Ralph H. Blum, screenwriter and author of several books, including *The New Book of Rune Sets*.

"Grateful people are happy people. The more things you are grateful for, the happier you will be."
Roy T. Bennett, thought leader and author of many books, including *The Light and the Heart*

"Happiness cannot be traveled to, owned, earned, worn or consumed. Happiness is the spiritual experience of living every minute with love, grace and gratitude."
Denis Waitley, American motivational speaker, writer and consultant, best-selling author of *The Psychology of Winning* and *The Winner's Edge*

"The happiest people on earth are not those who have robust bank accounts, or all the good things in this world; but they are those who truly embrace the attitude of gratitude. They are always focused, not on the things they are aspiring for, but for all the things God has used to bless their lives."
Sesan Kareem, speaker, pharmacist, life coach, author of books on self-development

"Of all the characteristics needed for both a happy and morally decent life, none surpasses gratitude. Grateful people are happier, and grateful people are more morally decent.
Dennis Prager, American conservative and nationally syndicated radio talk show host, columnist, author, and public speaker

"Success depends on your attitude, happiness depends on your gratitude."

Debasish Mridha, American physician, philosopher, poet seer, and author of S*weet Rhymes for Sweet Hearts*

"Miles and miles of smiles illustrated by the gratitude that creates them."

Paul Bradley Smith, cReAtIvE analytical intellectual and biographer.

"Gratitude paints little smiley faces on everything it touches."

Richelle E. Goodrich, American author, novelist, and poet, author of *Anyway* and *Wishes.*

"Gratefulness is the key to a happy life that we hold in our hands, because if we are not grateful, then no matter how much we have we will not be happy – because we will always want to have something else or something more."
Brother David Steindl-Rast, Catholic Benedictine monk, author of *Gratefulness, the Heart of Prayer.*

"A grateful mindset can set you free from the prison of disempowerment and the shackles of misery."
Steve Maraboli, author of *Unapologetically You: Reflections on Life and the Human Experience*

"It is impossible to be both grateful and depressed....The more I understand the mind and the human experience, the more I begin to suspect there is no such thing as unhappiness; there is only ungratefulness."
Steve Maraboli, author of *Life, the Truth, and Being Free*
and *Unapologetically Your: Reflections on Life and the Human Experience*

"Gratitude always comes into play; research shows that people are happier if they are grateful for the positive things in their lives, rather than worrying about what might be missing."

Dan Buettner, National Geographic Fellow and *New York Times* bestselling author of *Blue Zones: Lessons for Living Longer from the People Who've Lived the Longest*

"Expectation has brought me disappointment. Disappointment has brought me wisdom. Acceptance, gratitude and appreciation have brought me joy and fulfillment."

Rasheed Ogunlaru, life coach, speaker, and author of *Soul Trader*

RELATIONSHIPS

Feeling and expressing gratitude helps you have better relationships. Other people are more likely to want to be around you, because they feel your support, appreciation, and positive outlook. They recognize that you value them, and they experience your attitude of love and compassion. When you thank them or give them gifts of appreciation that helps to strengthen your bond with others, as well.

In response, others want to contribute to you and help you, and they can be instrumental to your successful achievements, because no one succeeds alone. We all depend on others, and when you act out of gratitude to others, they seek to join you and further your success.

The following quotes express these ideas.

"Let us be grateful to the people who make us happy; they are the charming gardeners who make our souls blossom."
Marcel Proust, French novelist, critic, and essayist, 1871-1922

"At times our own light goes out and is rekindled by a spark from another person. Each of us has cause to think with deep gratitude of those who have lighted the flame within us."
Albert Schweitzer, French-German theologian, philosopher, and physician. Author of several books including *Reverence for Life,* 1875-1965

"Be consistent in your dedication to showing your gratitude to others. Gratitude is a fuel, a medicine, and spiritual and emotional nourishment."
Steve Maraboli, author of *Life, the Truth, and Being Free*

"Gratitude is a mark of a noble soul and a refined character. We like to be around those who are grateful."
Joseph B. Wirthlin, American businessman, religious leader, and member of the Church of Jesus Christ of Latter-day Saints. 1917 - 2008

"Being in the habit of saying "Thank you," of making sure that people receive attention so they know you value them, of not presuming that people will always be there--This is a good habit, regardless...make sure to give virtual and actual high-fives to those who rock and rock hard."
Sarah Wendell, blogger and author, including *Everything I Know about Love I Learned from Romance Novels*

"Always recompense kindness with hearty love and gratitude."
Debasish Mridha, American physician, philosopher, poet seer, and author, including *Sweet Rhymes for Sweet Heart*

"Each day brings new opportunities, allowing you to constantly live with love – be there for others – bring a little light into someone's day. Be grateful and live each day to the fullest."
Roy T. Bennett, thought leader and author of many books, including *The Light and the Heart*

"Gratitude is the state of mind of thankfulness. As it is cultivated, we experience an increase in our 'sympathetic joy,' our happiness at another's happiness. Just as in the cultivation of compassion, we may feel the pain of others, so we may begin to feel their joy as well. And it doesn't stop there.
Stephen Levine, American poet, author, and teacher best known for his work on death and dying, including *A Year to Live.* 1937 – 2016.

"Blessed are those that can give without remembering and receive without forgetting."
Author Unknown

"There is as much greatness of mind in acknowledging a good turn, as in doing it."

Seneca, Roman philosopher, statesman, dramatist, and humorist, who wrote books, including *Letters from a Stoic to De Vita Beata,* 4 B.C.- 65 AD

"Two kinds of gratitude: The sudden kind we feel for what we take; the larger kind we feel for what we give."

Edwin Arlington Robinson, American poet, winner of three Pulitzer Prizes for his work, 1865 – 1935

"Be thankful for the efforts of people who worked hard to get you where you are; you should not take it for granted and treat them with indifference… Always remember people who have helped you along the way, and don't forget to lift someone up."
Roy T. Bennett, thought leader and author of many books, including *The Light and the Heart.*

"In normal life, we hardly realize how much more we receive than we give, and life cannot be rich without such gratitude. It is so easy to overestimate the importance of our own achievements compared with what we owe to the help of others."
Dietrich Bonhoeffer, German Lutheran pastor, theologian, anti-Nazi dissident, author of *Letters and Papers from Prison,* 1906-1945

"No one who achieves success does so without the help of others. The wise and confident acknowledge this help with gratitude."
Alfred North Whitehead, English mathematician and philosopher, best known as the defining figure of the process school of philosophy, 1861-1947

"When eating bamboo sprouts, remember the man who planted them."
Chinese Proverb

"How would your life be different if…you began each day by thanking someone who has helped you? Let today be the day…You make it a point to show your gratitude to others. Send a letter or card, make a call, send a text or email, tell them in person…do whatever you have to do to let them know you appreciate them."

   Steve Maraboli, author of *Unapologetically You: Reflections on Life and the Human Experience*

"The way to develop the best that is in a person is by appreciation and encouragement."
Charles Schwab, American investor, financial executive, philanthropist, and founder of the Charles Schwab Corporation in 1975

"When we become more fully aware that our success is due in large measure to the loyalty, helpfulness, and encouragement we have received from others, our desire grows to pass on similar gifts. Gratitude spurs us on to prove ourselves worthy of what others have done for us. The spirit of gratitude is a powerful energizer."
Winiferd A. Peterson, American author of *This Week* newspaper supplement and columnist for *Science of Mind* magazine

"Keep your eyes open and try to catch people in your company doing something right, then praise them for it."
Tom Hopkins, speaker, sales trainer, and author of multiple sales books including *How to Master the Art of Selling Anything*

"We love our partners for who they are, not for who they are not."
Aaron Lauritsen, author of *100 Days Drive: The Great North American Road Trip*

"Every morning when I wake up, I kiss her forehead as a symbol of gratitude and appreciation and she repays me back with a lovely smile."
M.F. Moonzajer, journalist, linguist, and author of *All About Feminism* and *A moment with God*

"We are told that people stay in love because of chemistry, or because they remain intrigued with each other, because of many kindnesses, because of luck. But part of it has got to be forgiveness and gratefulness."
Ellen Goodman, American journalist and Pulitzer Prize winning newspaper columnist

"Gratitude is a species of love, excited in us by some action of the person for whom we have it, and by which we believe that he has done some good to us, or at least that he has had the intention of doing so."

Renee Descartes, French philosopher, mathematician, and scientist, author of *Meditations on First Philosophy,* 1596-1650.

APPRECIATION

Being grateful also means appreciating yourself and others. We all need appreciation, because it means we are valued for who we are and what we do. It shows we are accepted and welcomed into a community with others, which is essential for mental health, since humans are a social species, where good relationship with others are critical.

Feeling this appreciation helps to give yourself and others a sense of pleasure and joy. It helps you feel a sense of satisfaction and peace for wherever you are in life, as you pursue other hopes and dreams.

It is important to reaffirm this sense of appreciation every day, not just at special times like Thanksgiving and Christmas, which are holidays for giving thanks and being thankful for receiving gifts. Then, too, you should experience appreciation for everything you see around you, as well as for just being alive. Additionally, you should not take anything you have for granted, because you may not recognize what you have not appreciated until after it is gone.

The following quotes express these ideas.

"Appreciation is the purest vibration that exists on the planet today."
Abraham Hicks, American inspirational speaker and co-author of the *Law of Attraction* series

"Whenever we are appreciative, we are filled with a sense of well-being and swept up by the feeling of joy."
M.J. Ryan, author of *Attitudes of Gratitude*, one of the creators of the best-selling series *Random Acts of Kindness*

Find the good and praise it."
Alex Haley, American writer and author of *Roots: The Saga of an American Family*

"The roots of all goodness lie in the soil of appreciation for goodness."
The 14th Dalai Lama, Buddhist Monk

"Appreciation is a wonderful thing. It makes what is excellent in others belong to us as well."
Voltaire, French Enlightenment writer, historian, and philosopher, 1694-1778

"Appreciation can make a day, even change a life. Your willingness to put it into words is all that is necessary."
Margaret Cousins, Irish-Indian educator, suffragist, and Theosophist, who established the All India Women's Conference

"The deepest craving of human nature is the need to be appreciated."
William James, American philosopher and psychologist, first educator to offer a psychology course in the United States, 1842-1910

"Whatever you appreciate and give thanks for will increase in your life."
Sanaya Roman, author of *Living with Joy: Keys to Personal Power and Spiritual Transformation*

"A sincere attitude of gratitude is a beatitude for secured altitudes. Appreciate what you have been given and you will be promoted higher."
Israelmore Ayivor, inspirational writer, blogger, LifeSkills Entrepreneur, and author of self-help and motivational books

"Learn to be thankful for what you already have, while you pursue all that you want."
Jim Rohn, American entrepreneur, author, and motivational speaker, 1930 – 2009

"Be grateful for what you already have while you pursue your goals."
Roy T. Bennett, thought leader and author of many books, including *The Light and the Heart*

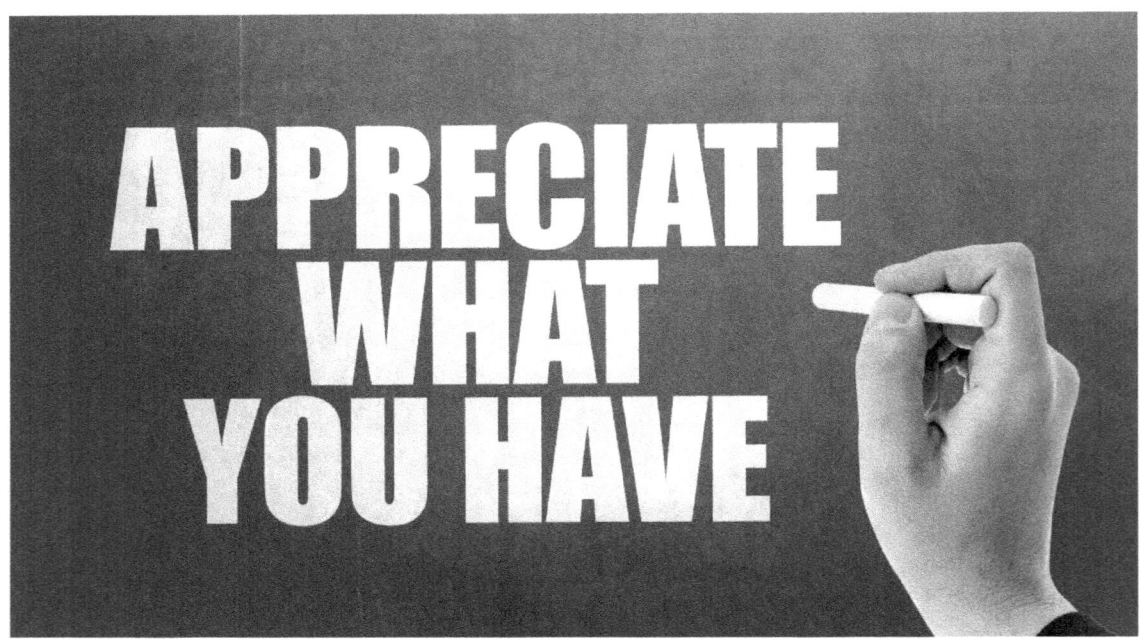

"Every day, in which you exist on earth, be filled with deep gratitude.
Lailah Gifty Akita, a Ghanaian, founder of the Smart Youth Volunteers Foundation, and author of *Think Great: Be Great!*

"When you arise in the morning, think of what a precious privilege it is to be alive – to breathe, to think, to enjoy, to love -- then make that day count."
Steve Maraboli, author of *Life, the Truth, and Being Free*

"Open your presents at Christmastime but be thankful year round for the gifts you receive."
Terri Guillemets, quotation anthologist, author of *A Renewed Outlook*

"Dance. Smile. Giggle. Marvel. TRUST. HOPE. LOVE. WISH. BELIEVE. Most of all, enjoy every moment of the journey, and appreciate where you are at this moment instead of always focusing on how far you have to go."
Mandy Hale, author of *The Single Woman: Life, Love, and a Dash of Sass*

"When it comes to life the critical thing is whether you take things for granted or take them with gratitude."
Gilbert K. Chesterton, English writer, poet, philosopher and author of *The Everlasting Man,* 1874-1936

"We can only be said to be alive in those moments when our hearts are conscious of our treasures.
Thornton Wilder, American playwright and Pulitzer Prize novelist, author of *The Bridge of San Luis Rey,* 1897-1975

"(Some people) have a wonderful capacity to appreciate again and again, freshly and naively, the basic goods of life, with awe, pleasure, wonder, and even ecstasy."
A.H. Maslow (1908 – 1970), American psychologist, creator of Maslow's Hierarchy of Needs

"When we focus on our gratitude, the tide of disappointment goes out and the tide of love rushes in."

Kristin Armstrong, author of *Ties that Bind* and *Happily Ever After*

"For the grateful, there is no room for disappointment. Each moment offers life."

Auliq-Ice, singer, songwriter, and author

"We don't truly appreciate what we have until it's gone…Be grateful for what you have now, and nothing should be taken for granted."

Roy T. Bennett, thought leader and author of many books, including *The Light and the Heart*

"Do not take anything for granted – not one smile or one person or one rainbow or one breath, or one night in your cozy bed."
Terri Guillemets, quotation anthologist, author of *A Renewed Outlook*

"Gratitude is the appreciation of things that are not deserved, earned or demanded – those wonderful things that we take for granted."
Renee Paule, author on philosophy, psychology, and self-help topics, including *On the Other Hand* and *Just Around the Bend*

"Whatever our individual troubles and challenges may be, it's important to pause every now and then to appreciate all that we have, on every level. We need to literally 'count our blessings,' give thanks for them, allow ourselves to enjoy them, and relish the experience of prosperity we already have."

Shakti Gawain, New Age and personal development author, books include *Creative Visualization* and *Developing Intuition*

"What if you gave someone a gift, and they neglected to thank you for it - would you be likely to give them another? Life is the same way. In order to attract more of the blessings that life has to offer, you must truly appreciate what you already have."
Ralph Marston, author and publisher of *The Daily Motivator*

"I look back with a mix of emotions: sadness for the people who are gone, nostalgia for times that have passed, but immense gratitude for the wonderful opportunities that came my way."
Dick Van Patten, American actor on the ABC television series *Eight Is Enough,* 1928-2015.

SAYING THANKS

Closely related to feeling and expressing appreciation is the notion of giving thanks to show that appreciation. While appreciation is more of an attitude or feeling, saying thanks is the act of telling others how much you appreciate and are thankful for something they have done. Say thanks to yourself, too.

Often thanks are said to God or to one's spiritual guides and teachers in the form of a prayer, which can be silent, spoken, written, or expressed alone or in a group. However you express your thanks, they are a way to consciously recognize what is good in your life, which can be anything you value.

This act of saying thank you can have a powerful effect – from feeling more peace and contentment to solidifying relationships to opening up new opportunities. You can always find something to be thankful for, even for something bad which didn't happen.

So get ready and find the time to say thank you for whatever you feel grateful for, whether that's in the form of a silent prayerful thank you, a statement to others, or a written letter or card telling others why you want to thank them.

The following quotes express these themes.

"If the only prayer you said in your whole life was, "thank you," that would be enough."

Meister Eckhart, German theologian, philosopher and mystic, 1260-1328

"'Thank You' is the best prayer that anyone could say. I say that one a lot. Thank you expresses the extreme gratitude, humility, and understanding."

Alice Walker, American novelist, writer, activist, and Pulitzer Prize winner for the novel *The Color Purple*

"When you start with thanksgiving, you will always end with praise. Be thankful, it grows."

TemitOpe Ibrahim, pastor, mentor, catalyst, and founder of the *Far Above Rubies* conference

"I would maintain that thanks are the highest form of thought, and that gratitude is happiness doubled by wonder."
Gilbert K. Chesterton, English writer, poet, philosopher and author of *The Everlasting Man*, 1874 -1936

"Gratitude means to recognize the good in your life, be thankful for whatever you have. Some people may not even have one of those things you consider precious to you (love, family, friends etc.) Each day give thanks for the gift of life. You are blessed."
Pablo, blogger and author on Good Reads

"Got no checkbooks, got no banks. Still I'd like to express my thanks – I've got the sun in the mornin' and the moon at night."
Irving Berlin, American composer and lyricist, 1888-1989.

"If you want to turn your life around, try thankfulness. It will change your life mightily."
Gerald Good, quotation author on Good Reads

"Eucharisteo – thanksgiving - always precedes the miracle."
Ann Voskamp, author of *One Thousand Gifts: A dare to Live Fully Right Where You are.*

"Give thanks for the life you live, for the love you have, for the happiness you give."
Laura, entrant in the November 2009 Quote Garden create your own quote contest on Twitter

Thankfulness creates gratitude which generates contentment that causes peace."

Todd Stocker, writer, speaker, and Executive Pastor at Trinity Congregation

"Let us rise up and be thankful, for if we didn't learn a lot today, at least we learned a little, and if we didn't learn a little, at least we didn't get sick, and if we got sick, at least we didn't die; so, let us all be thankful."

Buddha

"We must find time to stop and thank the people who make a difference in our lives."

John F. Kennedy, U.S. President, 1917-1963

"A little "thank you' that you will say to someone for a 'little favour' shown to you is a key to unlock the doors that hide unseen 'greater favours.' Learn to say 'thank you' and why not?"

Israelmore Ayivor, inspirational writer, blogger, LifeSkills Entrepreneur, and author of self-help and motivational books

"No duty is more urgent than that of returning thanks."
Unknown

"Everyone enjoys being acknowledged and appreciated. Sometimes even the simplest act of gratitude can change someone's entire day. Take the time to recognize and value the people around you and appreciate those who make a difference in your lives."

Roy T. Bennett, thought leader and author of many books, including *The Light and the Heart*

"Superficial social niceties are far different from the deep emotion of thanksgiving."

Alexandra Katehakis, author of *Mirror of Intimacy: Daily Reflections on Emotional and Erotic Intelligence*

"Not what we say about our blessings, but how we use them, is the true measure of our thanksgiving."

W.T. Purkiser, preacher, scholar, and author of *The Gifts of the Spirit,* active in the Church of the Nazarene, 1910 – 1992

"Thankfulness is the beginning of gratitude. Gratitude is the completion of thankfulness. Thankfulness may consist merely of words. Gratitude is shown in acts."

Henri Frederic Amiel, Swiss moral philosopher, poet, and critic, 1821- 1881

"God gave you a gift of 86,400 seconds today. Have you used one to say 'thank you?'

William A. Ward, American quotation writer of inspirational maxims, 1921 – 1994

"Be thankful that you don't already have everything you desire,
If you did, what would there be to look forward to?
Be thankful when you don't know something
For it gives you the opportunity to learn.
Be thankful for the difficult times.
During those times you grow.
Be thankful for your limitations
Because it will build your strength and character.
Be thankful when you're tired and weary
Because it means you've made a difference.
It is easy to be thankful for the good things.
A life of rich fulfillment comes to those who are
Also thankful for the setbacks.
GRATITUDE can turn a negative into a positive.
Find a way to be thankful for your troubles
And they can become your blessings."
Author Unknown

ACHIEVEMENT

Gratitude can help you achieve what you want, even greatness. A key reason gratitude can do this is the benefits that a positive, contented attitude brings into your life. One benefit is better relationships with people who want to help you. Also, this outlook can inspire you to be more committed to your work and more productive. Then these good results contribute to creating a virtuous cycle, in which more benefits trigger even more benefits to come into your life.

For example, more productivity leads to more profits which lead to more productivity leading to even more profits, and the cycle continues with further production and profits. Or relationships expand in an ever increasing network. Whatever you can think of, a virtuous cycle inspires further growth, while gratitude results in its own virtuous cycle of more and more benefits, so you can better achieve what you want.

Thus, continue to be appreciative and thankful for whatever you achieve in life, and that attitude will help feel good, stay positive, and achieve much more. Even if you encounter disappointment that will be a source of learning you can be thankful for, since that will lead you to develop new alternatives and plans.

The following quotes express these ideas.

"An attitude of gratitude brings great things."
Yogi Bhajan, yogi, spiritual teacher, and entrepreneur, founder of the Happy, Healthy, Holy Organization, 1929-2004.

"Those who have the ability to be grateful are the ones who have the ability to achieve greatness."
Steve Maraboli, author of *Life, the Truth, and Being Free*

"Your attitude of gratitude will bring you altitude in business and multitude in blessings."
Farshad Asl, entrepreneur, leadership coach, speaker, and Regional Director at Bankers Life

"Be thankful for what you have; you'll end up having more. If you concentrate on what you don't have, you will never, ever have enough."
Oprah Winfrey, American media entrepreneur, talk show host, actress, producer, and philanthropist

"Give thanks for a little and you will find a lot."
The Hausa of Nigeria

"Who does not thank for little will not thank for much."
Estonian Proverb

"Cultivate the habit of being grateful for every good thing that comes to you, and to give thanks continuously. And because all things have contributed to your advancement, you should include all things in your gratitude."
Ralph Waldo Emerson, American essayist, lecturer, poet, 1803-1882

"Gratitude turns disappointment into lessons learned, discoveries made, alternatives explored, and new plans set in motion."
Auliq-Ice, singer, songwriter, and author

"Saying thanks to the world and acknowledging your own accomplishments is a great way to feel good and stay positive."
Rachel Robins, author of *How To Feel Good About Yourself – Boost Your Confidence & Tackle Low Self Esteem*

"What separates privilege from entitlement is gratitude."
Brene Brown, American scholar, author, public speaker, and author of *Rising Strong*

"I'm very lucky to be able to do what I do for a living and giving back is a way for me to express my gratitude. I'm so lucky to be in a position to help people, and that's appealing to me."
PewDiePie, Swedish web-based comedian and video producer

CONTENTMENT AND ACCEPTANCE

Another benefit of feeling gratitude is the experience of contentment you feel on accepting what is. This attitude also helps you to stay focused on what you are gaining in the present, even though you gained that through what you did in the past. This way, you feel more satisfaction and enjoyment in the here and now, and you don't look back with regrets on anything that happened in the past.

In turn, this positive attitude can help you better prepare for what is to come by complimenting yourself for who you are and what you have done. As a result, you feel more confident about your ability to do what you hope to do. Moreover, experiencing gratitude helps you feel content about whatever you have accomplished, and it reminds you that it is better to complete something. so it is done rather than trying to make it perfect, which can be an impossible standard to meet. Rather you want to be content and accept who you are and what you have done, not judge yourself against much higher impossible to reach standards, so you put yourself down. As gratitude teaches, honor what has happened in the past, appreciate and enjoy the present, and do not use hindsight to let your inner critic judge yourself.

The following quotes express these ideas.

"True happiness is to enjoy the present…The greatest blessings of mankind are within us and within our reach. A wise man is content with his lot, whatever it may be, without wishing for what he has not."
Seneca, Roman philosopher, statesman, dramatist, 4 B.C.- 65 A.D.

"He is a wise man who does not grieve for the things which he has not, but rejoices for those which he has."
Epictetus, Greek-speaking Stoic philosopher, 55 A.D. – 135 A.D

"Gratitude and love are always multiplied when you give freely. It is an infinite source of contentment and prosperous energy."
Jim Fargiano, author of *The Spoken Words of Spirit: Lessons from the Other Side*

"Give thanks, because contentment only grows when you shower upon it gratefulness."

Hasan Gopalani, entrant in the November 2009 Quote Garden create your own quote contest on Twitter

"It's up to us to choose contentment and thankfulness now – and to stop imagining that we have to have everything perfect before we'll be happy."

Joanna Gaines, author of *The Magnolia Story*

"The struggle ends when the gratitude begins."
Neale Donald Walsch, American author of the series, *Conversations with God*

"I may not be where I want to be but I'm thankful for not being where I used to be."
Habeeb Akande, British-born writer and historian of Nigerian descent, author of *Illuminating the Darkness*

"Be grateful for what you already have while you pursue your goals. If you aren't grateful for what you already have, what makes you think you would be happy with more...Being grateful does not mean that everything is necessarily good. It just means that you can accept it as a gift."

Roy T. Bennett, thought leader and author of many books, including *The Light and the Heart*

"I have learned over a period of time to be almost unconsciously grateful—as a child is—for a sunny day, blue water, flowers in a vase, a tree turning red. I have learned to be glad at dawn and when the sky is dark. Only children and a few spiritually evolved people are born to feel gratitude as naturally as they breathe, without even thinking. Most of us come to it step by painful step, to discover that gratitude is a form of acceptance."

Faith Baldwin, author of *Many Windows, Seasons of the Heart*

LEARNING AND EXPERIENCE

Still another virtue of feeling gratitude is that it reminds us to view everything that happens as an experience to learn or gain from in some way, so we can have even better experiences in the future. Therefore, we should feel grateful for even difficult, challenging experiences, because they help us grow and move on. They even open up opportunities for us to experience some of the best things that occur in our life, which wouldn't have occurred had we not had to overcome and grow due to a difficulty we encountered.

The following quotes express these ideas.

"Be thankful for everything that happens in your life; it's all an experience."

Roy T. Bennett, thought leader and author of many books, including *The Light and the Heart*

"Gratitude gets us through the hard stuff…Gratitude always leaves us looking at God and away from dread."

Max Lucado, author of *You'll Get Through This: Hope and Help for Your Turbulent Times*.

"Some of the best things that have happened to us wouldn't have happened to us, if it weren't for some of the worst things that have ever happened to us."
Mokokoma Mokhonoana, philosopher, social critic, graphic designer, and writer of thought-provoking essays and books

"Be grateful for the situations in your life that may seem chaotic in the present moment, and realize that, in the greater scheme of things, chaos is Spirit giving you an opportunity…or possibly, pushing you to move, grow and be in the flow."
Alaric Hutchinson, author of *Living Peace*

FAITH

Having gratitude is a core principle of all religious faiths. Expressing gratitude is viewed as a way to honor and worship God or the saints, guides, and teachers associated with that faith. It shows you accept and appreciate this higher power beyond yourself, and you accept whatever you have been given in life. In turn, this outlook contributes to your sense of peace and contentment, while giving you more energy to go forward with a positive attitude, because you feel the support of God or the saints, guides, teachers, or the universe itself.

Being grateful can also help you feel better about any trials and tribulations in you encounter, since you can see them as a test or challenge for you to grow even stronger, due to what you have learned or gained in overcoming this hardship.

The following quotes express these ideas.

"Gratitude is the fairest blossom which springs from the soul."
Henry Ward Beecher, clergyman, 1813-1887

"Gratitude is the sign of noble souls."
Aesop, Greek fabulist and storyteller, credited with a number of fables known as *Aesop's Fables,* 620-564 B.C.

"Saying thank you is more than good manners. It is good spirituality."
Alfred Painter, frequently quoted author of this quote

"Gratitude is a form of worship in its own right, as it implies the acceptance of a power greater than yourself."
Steven Richards, parishioner at the First United Methodist Church in Richardson, Texas

"To speak gratitude is courteous and pleasant, to enact gratitude is generous and noble, but to live gratitude is to touch Heaven."
Johannes A Gaertner, aesthetician, art educational theorist, and art history professor at Lafayette College in Pennsylvania, 1912 – 1996

"Let gratitude be the pillow upon which you kneel to say your nightly prayer. And let faith be the bridge you build to overcome evil and welcome good."

Maya Angelou, American poet, memoirist, and civil rights activist, 1928-2014

"When I wake up each morning, my first thought is thanks be to God."
Laila Gifty Akita, a Ghanaian and founder of the Smart Youth Volunteers Foundation

"More miracles occur from Gratitude and Forgiveness than anything else."
Philip H. Friedman, author of *The Forgiveness Solution: The Whole-Body Rx for Finding True Happiness, Abundant Love, and Inner Peace*

"He who does not reflect his life back to God in gratitude does not know himself."
Albert Schweitzer, French-German theologian, philosopher, physician, and author of several books including *Reverence for Life: The Words of Albert Schweitzer,* 1875-1965

"When God is our Holy Father, sovereignty, holiness, omniscience, and immutability do not terrify us; they leave us full of awe and gratitude."
Ravi Zacharias Indian-born Canadian-American Christian apologist, and author of several Christian books including *Can Men Live Without God?*

"Life-giving ministry flows from lives that are full of gratitude to God, not with an expectation from others."
Christopher L. Heuertz, author of *Friendship at the Margins: Discovering Mutuality in Service and Mission*

"Gratitude bestows reverence, allowing us to encounter everyday epiphanies, those transcendent moments of awe that change forever how we experience life and the world."
John Milton, English poet, polemicist, man of letters, and civil servant for the Commonwealth of England, 1608 – 1674

"When you thank GOD for what you have, it means you appreciate and value what's in your hands. And when you value what's in your hands it will open up its window."

TemitOpe Ibrahim, pastor, mentor, catalyst and founder of the *Far Above Rubies* conference

"Everything we do should be a result of our gratitude for what God has done for us."

Lauryn Hill, American singer, songwriter, record producer and actress

"Perhaps nothing helps us make the movement from our little selves to a larger world than remembering God in gratitude. Such a perspective puts God in view in all of life, not just in the moments we set aside for worship or spiritual disciplines; not just in the moments when life seams easy.

Henri Nouwen, Dutch Catholic priest, professor, writer, and theologian, 1932 – 1996

"I truly believe we can either see the connections, celebrate them, and express gratitude for our blessings, or we can see life as a string of coincidences that have no meaning or connection."

Mike Ericksen, author of *Upon Destiny's Song*

"Can you see the holiness in those things you take for granted – a paved road or a washing machine? If you concentrate on finding what is good in every situation you will discover that your life will suddenly be filled with gratitude, a feeling that nurtures the soul."
Rabbi Harold Kushner, American Conservative rabbi and author of *When Bad Things Happen to Good People*

"In the silence of children, God exists, directing their thoughts and sending us subtle reminders as not forgetting gratitude even in the list of little."
Chinonye J. Chidolue, creative writer, poet, deep thinker, and inspirationalist

"Love of God is pure when joy and suffering inspire an equal degree of gratitude."
Simone Weil, author *Gravity of Grace*

"The unthankful heart... discovers no mercies; but let the thankful heart sweep through the day and, as the magnet finds the iron, so it will find, in every hour, some heavenly blessings."
Henry Ward Beecher, clergyman, 1813-1887

"I see the glass half full and thank God for what I have."
Ana Monnar, elementary school teacher and author of *Express Yourself 101 Kaleidoscope Volume 3*

"Oh Infinite Father, I'm grateful to Thee. For the moon and the stars and deep rolling sea; For beauties of nature, where e'er they may be…For handclasp of friends, so firm and so true; For sunrise and sunset and glistening dew; the fleecy white clouds and the Heavens, so blue; for these wonderful gifts, dear Lord, I thank you!

Gertrude T. Buckingham, author of many poems, including *Poems at Random,* 1880-1957

"I humbly thank the gods benign, For all the blessings that are mine…The morning drips her dew for me, Noon spreads an opal canopy. Home-bound, the drifting cloud-crafts rest Where sunset ambers all the west; Soft o'er the poppy-fields of sleep, The drowsy winds of dreamland creep. What idle things are wealth and fame Beside the treasures one could name!

Robert Loveman, American poet, 1864-1923

ABUNDANCE

Gratitude is also a source of abundance. While abundance is sometimes associated with achievement, since it can result from successfully achieving something, it can simply come into one's life, often due to positive thinking, belief, and faith. For example, many writers suggest that just expressing gratitude and giving thanks can bring abundance into your life.

How? Because having a grateful outlook will attract abundance to you. Perhaps one reason this approach works is that being grateful attracts successful people to you, and when you give freely to others, they reciprocate so you end up getting more than you give. Thus, the more you give, the more you might eventually get.

The following quotes express these ideas.

"Thanksgiving creates abundance"
Ann Voskamp, author of *One Thousand Gifts: A Dare to Live Fully Right Where You Are*

"Acknowledging the good that you already have in your life is the foundation for all abundance."
Eckhart Tolle, German-born resident of Canada, best known as the author of *The Power of Now* and *A New Earth: Awakening to your Life's Purpose*.

"Gratitude unlocks the door of opportunities, blessing, greatness, and prosperity. Gratitude is your key to a worthy life."
Sesan Kareem, speaker, pharmacist, life coach, and author of books on self-development

"Gratitude builds a bridge to abundance."
Roy T. Bennett, thought leader and author of many books, including *The Light and the Heart*

"A generous heart filled with gratitude is a magnet for abundance … The best way to achieve great success is to learn from wise people. Use them extensively with love, gratitude, and humility."
Debasish Mridha, American physician, philosopher, poet seer, and author of S*weet Rhymes for Sweet Hearts*

"If you count all your assets, you always show a profit."
Robert Quillen, American journalist and humorist, 1887 – 1948

"When you are grateful, fear disappears and abundance appears."
Anthony Robbins, American businessman, inspirational speaker, and author, including *Unlimited Power* and *Unleash the Power Within*

"Summoning gratitude is a sure way to get our life back on track. Opening our eyes to affirm gratitude grows the garden of our inner abundance, just as standing close to a fire eventually warms our heart."
Alexandra Katehakis, author of *Mirror of Intimacy: Daily Reflections on Emotional and Erotic Intelligence*

"Gratitude is riches. Complaint is poverty."
Doris Day, retired American actress and singer

"In ordinary life, we hardly realize that we receive a great deal more than we give, and that it is only with gratitude that life becomes rich."
Dietrich Bonhoeffer, German Lutheran pastor, theologian, anti-Nazi dissident, and author of *Letters and Papers from Prison,* 1906-1945

"Gratitude is a currency that we can mint for ourselves, and spend without fear of bankruptcy."
Fred De Witt Van Amburgh, cartographer and artist, 1630 – 1706

"I have come to realize that truly rich people are rich not because they are frugal or they chose to be frugal, but because they are so grateful, contented and full of self-worth that they don't have to prove anything to anyone with material possessions. This way, they appear frugal."
Jan Mckingley Hilado, author of *Rich Real Radical: 40 Lessons from a Magna Cum Laude and a College Drop Out*

"When you are grateful, fear disappears and abundance appears."
Anthony Robbins, American businessman, inspirational speaker, and author, including *Unlimited Power* and *Unleash the Power Within*

FUTURE BENEFITS

Gratitude will bring you a better future, too. Besides gaining abundance in the form of wealth, this future can result in you receiving more of whatever you most value. This can include more friends, better family relationships, more adventures and experiences, whatever you want to be and do. Consider what you will gain like a future bucket list, except you don't have to kick the bucket to realize your hopes and dreams.

These future benefits can include all sorts of things – better relationships, work opportunities, more money – whatever you want, because an attitude of gratitude can bring you more blessings of every sort and enable you to achieve much more than in your present circumstances. By contrast, if you aren't grateful for what you have, you will block these future benefits from coming into your life.

The following quotations express these themes.

"Count your blessings as the more you are grateful for what you have the more there is to be grateful for."
Pravin Agarwal, software engineer from India and author of *8 Course Meal for the Soul*

"Feeling grateful or appreciative of someone in your life actually attracts more of the things that you appreciate and value into your life."
Christiane Northrup, obstetrician, gynecologist, and advocate for women's health

"Great things happen to those who don't stop believing, trying, learning, and being grateful."
Roy T. Bennett, thought leader and author of many books, including *The Light and the Heart*

"What you focus on expands, and when you focus on the goodness in your life, you create more of it. Opportunities, relationships, even money flowed my way when I learned to be grateful no matter what happened in my life."

Oprah Winfrey, American media entrepreneur, talk show host, actress, producer, and philanthropist

"Develop an attitude of gratitude, and give thanks for everything that happens to you, knowing that every step forward is a step toward achieving something bigger and better than your current situation."

Brian Tracy, Canadian-born American motivational public speaker and self-development author of many books, including *The Psychology of Achievement*

"If a fellow isn't thankful for what he's got, he isn't likely to be thankful for what he's going to get."
Frank A. Clark, American politician and lawyer, 1860 – 1936

"Nothing new can come into your life unless you are grateful for what you already have."
Michael Bernard Beckwith, American New Thought minister, author, and founder of the Agape International Spiritual Center

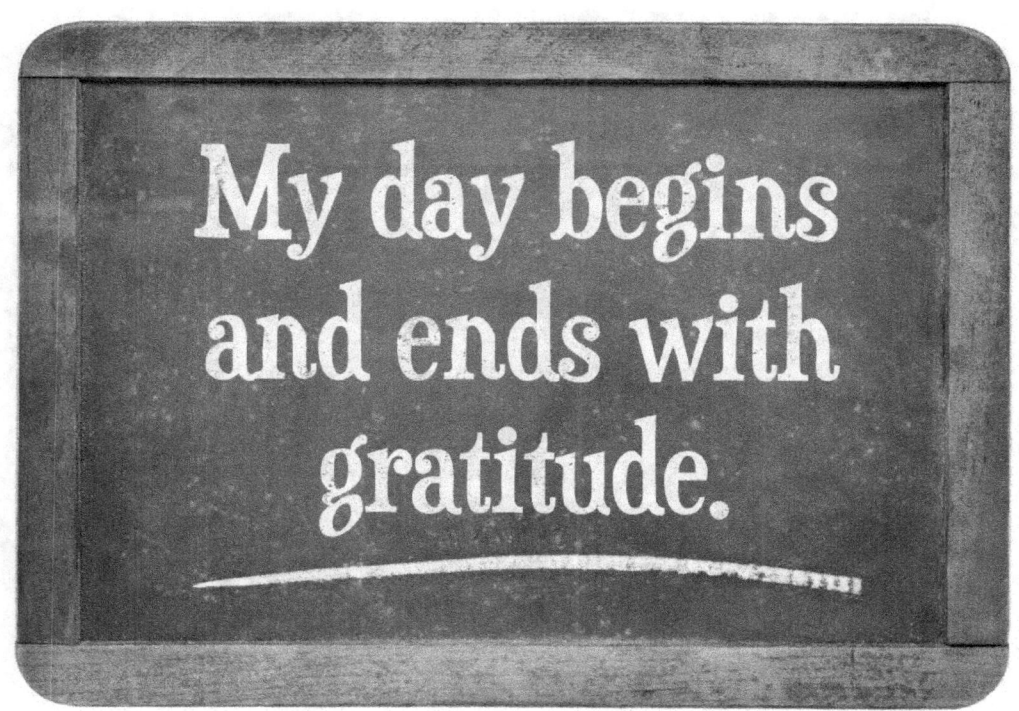

"Things turn out best for people who make the best of the way things turn out."
John Wooden, American basketball player and coach, 1910 – 2010

"Enjoy the little things, for one day you may look back and realize they were the big things."
Robert Brault, free-lance writer and author of *Round Up the Usual Subjects: Thoughts on Just about Everything*

GIVING

Giving is another essential component of expressing your gratitude. You give to others because of something they have done, which makes you feel thankful, so out of reciprocity you want to give back. Alternatively, you give out of a spirit of generosity, and in return, immediately, or in the future, you get back from the person you have given to or from others. In fact, often this giving is returned three fold, tenfold, or more, because of the spirit of giving and generosity in your heart. So giving to others in gratitude is a source of abundance for you.

Sometimes this value of giving is expressed as a form of gaining a blessing for yourself and others. Or it may be described as a way of achieving a balance in life, whereby the acts of giving and receiving are on a kind of scale. As you give, so shall you receive; or in accordance with the law of karma, each action brings about certain consequences, so if you give, you receive back certain benefits as a result of your generous act.

The following quotes deal with these themes.

"When we give cheerfully and accept gratefully, everyone is blessed."
Maya Angelou, American poet, memoirist, and civil rights activist, 1928-2014

"Life works with balance. If you give and receive out of giving, you create a balance with a life. You serve life, before you expect life to serve you."
Roshan Sharma, author of *The Reflection of Ultimate Truth: The Guide to the Path of Self-Realization*

HAVING A POSITIVE ATTITUDE

Being grateful is also closely linked with having a positive attitude, whether that attitude leads to feeling gratitude or living life with gratitude leads to having a positive state of mind.

Often the ideas of having a positive outlook and feeling and expressing gratitude are linked together, so you should exhibit both and will have positive experiences in return. You will feel happier, too, by thinking positive thoughts and turning any adversities into experiences to feel thankful for, since they become opportunities for discovery, learning, and growth.

In other words, by being positive, by focusing on what's good in your life, not on the negative, your feelings of gratitude can transform the bad into good, the coal into diamonds. That transformation happens because you see whatever challenges you encounter as a blessing, not a curse.

The following quotes deal with these themes.

"Be grateful for the day and the day will be grateful for you. Stay positive and everything else around you will respond in kind."

TemitOpe Ibrahim, pastor, mentor, catalyst, and founder of the *Far Above Rubies* conference

"Start each day with a positive thought and a grateful heart... When one has a grateful heart, life is so beautiful."

Roy T. Bennett, thought leader and author of many books, including *The Light and the Heart*

"When you focus on gratitude, positive things flow in more readily, making you seem even more grateful."
Lissa Rankin, author of *Mind Over Medicine: Scientific Proof that You Can Heal Yourself.*

"Gratitude always comes into play; research shows that people are happier if they are grateful for the positive things in their lives, rather than worrying about what might be missing."
Dan Buettner, National Geographic Fellow and *New York Times* bestselling author of *Blue Zones: Lessons for Living Longer from the People Who've Lived the Longest*

"Gratitude is an art of painting an adversity into a lovely picture."
Kak Sri, winner of the November 2010 Quote Garden create your own quote contest on Twitter

"Reflect upon your present blessings, of which every man has plenty; not on our past misfortunes, of which all men have some."
Charles Dickens, English writer and social critic, 1812 – 1860

"In order to complete our amazing life journey successfully, it is vital that we turn each and every dark tar into a pearl of wisdom, and find the blessing in every curse."
Anthon St. Maarten, international psychic medium and destiny coach, author of *Divine Living: The Essential Guide to Your True Destiny*

"Some people grumble that roses have thorns; I am grateful that thorns have roses."
Alphonse Karr, French critic, journalist, and novelist, author of *A Tour Round My Garden,* 1808-1890.

"The problem that we have with a victim mentality is that we forget to see the blessings of the day. Because of this, our spirit is poisoned instead of nourished."
Steve Maraboli, author of *Unapologetically Your: Reflections on Life and the Human Experience*

APPRECIATING LIFE

Gratitude is not just about being thankful for particular things, experiences, or opportunities but feeling grateful for life generally. Living out of gratitude becomes a way of always living your life rather than only expressing this attitude at times. You should be grateful for just being alive.

For example, you should feel gratitude for everything, and the more you practice this in daily life, the more you will feel a part of the whole world. You should also embrace each day with gratitude and remember that you are like a traveler passing through on your life's journey, where you can keep nothing in the end. Thus, you should be grateful for what you have in the here and now, since life is the ultimate gift, and you should be thankful for all the opportunities and experiences you have along the way. Plus be thankful for the natural world you see around you as you travel through life. And when you encounter hardships or see the hardships of others, think of what you can be grateful for, because that will contribute to your happiness, too.

The following quotes deal with these themes.

"Express gratitude for every little thing."
Debasish Mridha, American physician, philosopher, poet seer, and author of S*weet Rhymes for Sweet Hearts*

"To live, to truly live, one must consider each and every thing a blessing."
Kamand Kojouri, writer and poet

"The more grateful we are, the more we practice this in our everyday lives, the more connected we become to the universe around us."
Stephen Richards, blogger and creator of the *Cosmic Ordering Newsletter*

"Grace isn't a little prayer you chant before receiving a meal, it's a way to live."
Jacqueline Winspear, mystery writer and author of the Maisie Dobbs series

"The longer you linger in gratitude, the more you draw your new life to you. For gratitude is the ultimate state of receivership."
Dr. Joe Dispenza, author, researcher, chiropractor, and lecturer

"Breath is the finest gift of nature. Be grateful for this wonderful gift."
Amit Ray, Indian spiritual master and author of *Awakening Inner Guru: The Path of Realizing the God Within*

"One should be glad for every breath one can take in this world."
Marty Rubin, writer and author of *The Boiled Frog Syndrome*

As each day comes to us refreshed and anew, so does my gratitude renew itself daily. The breaking of the sun over the horizon is my grateful heart dawning upon a blessed world."

Terri Guillemets, quotation anthologist, author of *A Renewed Outlook*

"Regardless of sunshine or rain, be thankful for another great day…and treat life as the ultimate gift…We only live once…I am saying that so you can cherish each moment in your life and be grateful that you are here and you are special."

Pablo, blogger and author on Good Reads

"Nothing in life is yours to keep – not your children, not your friends and family, not your lover, not your material possessions, not your youth and vitality, not your struggles (which is great news) or successes, not your body and not even your life. Everything in life is given to you for a short period of time, to enjoy, to learn from, to appreciate and to love, but never to keep.
Luminita D. Saviuc, blogger and the founder of Purpose Fairy

"Gratitude is the ability to experience life as a gift. It liberates us from the prison of self-preoccupation."
John Ortberg, evangelical Christian author, speaker, senior pastor at an evangelical church, and author of *When the Game Is Over, It All Goes Back in the Box*

"Nature's beauty is a gift that cultivates appreciation and gratitude."
Louie Schwartzberg, American film director, producer, cinematographer, pioneer in high-end time-lapse cinematography

"Give yourself a gift of five minutes of contemplation in awe of everything you see around you. Go outside and turn your attention to the many miracles around you. This five-minute-a-day regimen of appreciation and gratitude will help you to focus your life in awe."
Wayne Dyer, American philosopher, self-help author, motivational speaker, and author of *A Perfect World*, 1940 – 2015

"The world has enough beautiful mountains and meadows, spectacular skies and serene lakes. It has enough lush forests, flowered fields, and sandy beaches. It has plenty of stars and the promises of a new sunshine and sunset every day. What the world needs more of its people to appreciate and enjoy it."
Michael Josephson, speaker, lecturer, and founder of the nonprofit Joseph and Edna Josephson Institute of Ethics in Los Angeles.

"Sometimes we should express our gratitude for the small and simple things like the scent of the rain, the taste of your favorite food, or the sound of a loved one's voice."
Joseph B. Wirthlin, American businessman, religious leader and member of the Quorum of the Twelve Apostles of The Church of Jesus Christ of Latter-day Saints, 1917 - 2008

"Most of us forget to take time for wonder, praise, and gratitude until it is almost too late. Gratitude is a many-colored quality, reaching in all directions. It goes out for small things and for large; it is a God-ward going."
Faith Baldwin, American author of over 100 romance and fiction novels, including *Many Windows, Seasons of the Heart,* 1893 – 1978

"You say grace before meals. All right. But I say grace before the concert and the opera, and grace before the play and pantomime, and grace before I open a book, and grace before sketching, painting, swimming, fencing, boxing, walking, playing, dancing, and grace before I dip the pen in the ink."

Gilbert K. Chesterton, English writer, poet, philosopher, and author of *The Everlasting Man*

"Gratitude for the seemingly insignificant – a seed – this plants the giant miracle."

Ann Voskamp, American author of *One Thousand Gifts: A Dare to Live Fully Right Where You Are*

"My prayer is an attitude of pure gratitude for having the opportunity to experience life on this earth with all its pain, heartache, worry, and turmoil; coupled with this gratitude is the thankfulness for just having the opportunity to have lived."

David W. Earle, business coach, author of *Red Roses 'n Pinstripes*

"Each day brings new opportunities, allowing you to constantly live with love – be there for others – bring a little light into someone's day. Be grateful and live each day to the fullest."

Roy T. Bennett, thought leader and author of many books, including *The Light and the Heart*

"Those who are truly grateful are deeply moved by the privilege of living."

Auliq-Ice, singer, songwriter, and author

"…I was thinking that gratitude is too much absent in our lives now, and we need it back, even if it only takes the form of acknowledging the blue of a bowl against the red of cranberries."

Elizabeth Berg, American novelist of several books, including *Open House*

"Deeply happy people are even thankful for the trials and tragedies they pass through."

Auliq-Ice, singer, songwriter, and author

"When I think of how many people in this world have it worse than I do, I realize just how blessed I really am…"
Shannan Lea, author of *Eish! London*

"It has been said that life has treated me harshly; and sometimes I have complained in my heart because many pleasures of human experience have been withheld from me…if much has been denied me, much, very much, has been given me..."
Helen Keller, American political activist, lecturer, and author of *The Open Door*, 1880 – 1968

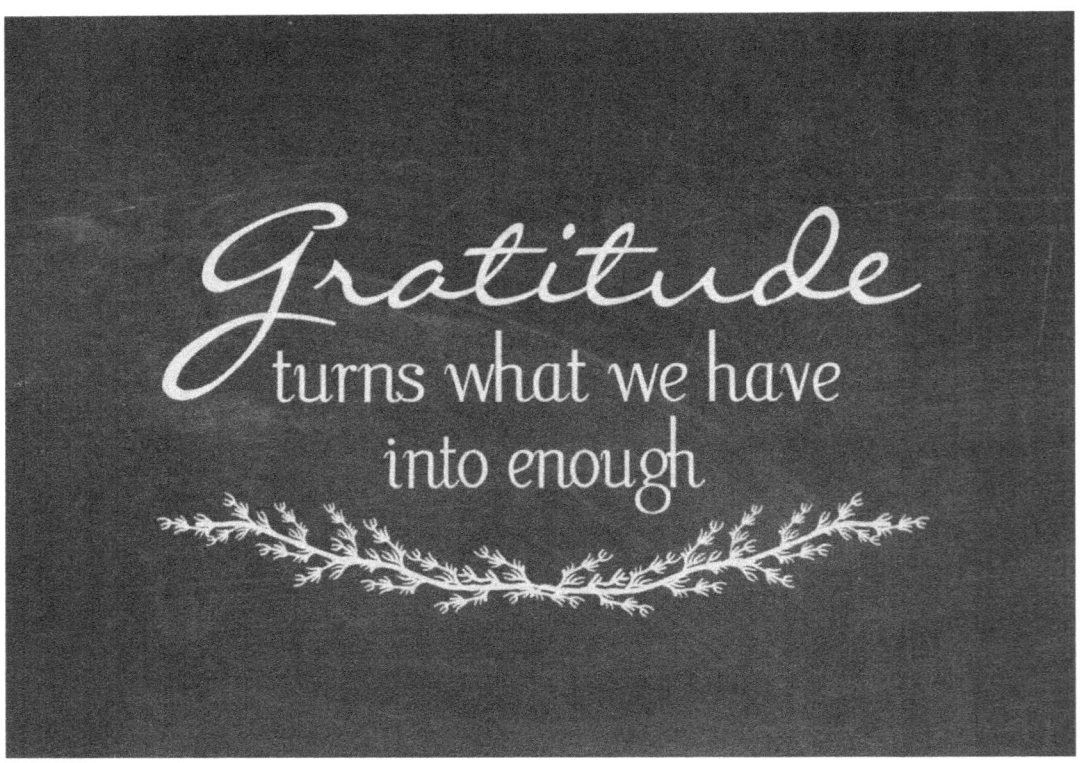

ANIMAL EMOTIONS

As another indicator of the importance of gratitude, consider that animals, too, express gratitude. Sometimes they show even more of this to others than humans do. They express this gratitude in many ways, including showing love and loyalty to those they rely on for companionship and trust.

So if animals can express gratitude, shouldn't humans be able to do the same?

The following quotes express these ideas.

"If having a soul means being able to feel love and loyalty and gratitude, then animals are better off than a lot of humans."
James Herriot, British veterinary surgeon, writer, and author of *All Creatures Great and Small,* 1916 – 1995

"Does not the gratitude of the dog put to shame any man who is ungrateful to his benefactors?"

Saint Basil, Greek bishop of Caesarea Mazaca in Asia Minor, known for his care of the poor and underprivileged, and author of many books including *On the Holy Spirit*, 330-390

PEOPLE WHO ARE NOT GRATEFUL

Unfortunately, those who are not grateful have a difficult time of it. They lack the feelings of comfort the grateful experience, and they see only limits, whereas the grateful see possibilities and potential everywhere. They feel dissatisfaction about their lot in life and are often unhappy, fearful, and angry, because they focus on what's negative or wrong and not what is satisfying and works well. All that negativity diminishes them, too, so they undermine their own efforts to gain success.

In short, their lack of gratitude brings them all measure of hardship and difficulties, because of the laws of attraction and cause and consequences.

The following quotes express these themes.

"There is no greater difference between men than between grateful and ungrateful."
R.H. Blyth, author of *Haiku: Eastern Culture*

"The soul that gives thanks can find comfort in everything; the soul that complains can find comfort in nothing."
Hannah Whitall Smith, activist during the Women's suffrage movement and author, including *The Christian's Secret of a Happy Life*, 1832 – 1911

"Gratitude also opens your eyes to the limitless potential of the universe, while dissatisfaction closes your eyes to it."
Stephen Richards, author of several self-help books including *Think Your Way to Success: Let Your Dreams Run Free*

"Ungrateful people forget what they are not grateful for."
Ana Monnar, elementary school teacher and author of *Express Yourself 101 Kaleidoscope Volume 3*

"But the value of gratitude does not consist solely in getting you more blessings in the future. Without gratitude you cannot long keep from dissatisfied thought regarding things as they are…Many people who order their lives rightly in all other ways are kept in poverty by their lack of gratitude."
Wallace Wattles, American author of many books including *The Science of Getting Rich*, 1860 – 1911

"Those who are too arrogant to say thank you find boredom in life. They are often depressed, unhappy and live an empty life…There are three things that stop people from becoming their best, 'fear' 'anger' and 'greed.' The antidote to fear is action, the cure for anger is gratitude, and the medicine to greed is love."
Sesan Kareem, speaker, pharmacist, life coach, and author of books on self-development

"It is from this lack of true gratitude that we become sad. We have told ourselves over and over that we aren't happy. That our lives aren't good. That we're no good."

S.R. Crawford, author of *From My Suffering: 25 Ways to Break the Chains of Anxiety, Depression and Stress*

HUMILITY

Finally, a key principle of having gratitude is showing humility. Even as good things flow into your life and you experience abundance, you should remain humble. Otherwise you may destroy your feelings of gratitude, and others may see your show of being grateful as insincere. Then, too, due to the laws of attraction and cause and effect, you may undermine whatever gifts you have gotten through not showing gratitude. In other words, as they say: "Pride goeth before a fall," and that can result in your losing whatever you have not been grateful for.

The following quotes reflect these themes.

"Gratitude…staying humble when fate smiles on you."
Quintas Nienaber, entry into the November 2010 Quote Garden create your own quote contest on Twitter

"Love casts out fear, and gratitude can conquer pride."
Louisa May Alcott, American novelist and poet, best known for the novel *Little Women,* 1832 – 1888

"We may spoil gratitude as we offer it, by insisting on its recognition. To receive honestly is the best thanks for a good thing."
George MacDonald, author of *Mary Marston,* 1824 – 1905

"Meekness implies a spirit of gratitude as opposed to an attitude of self-sufficiency, and an acknowledgment of a greater power beyond oneself, a recognition of God, and an acceptance of his commandments."
Gordon B. Hinckley, American religious leader, 15th President of The Church of Jesus Christ of Latter-day Saints, and author of *Cultivating an Attitude of Happiness and a Spirit of Optimism,* 1910-2008.

APPLYING THE GRATITUDE OUTLOOK IN YOUR LIFE

As the previous sections have described, having gratitude for what you receive and experience can be very fulfilling for you personally, as well as help you have better relationships with others and be more successful in business.

Personally, feeling grateful can help you feel happier, because you appreciate whatever is happening in your life, and you can better deal with any adversities by seeing them as learning and growing experiences rather than feeling regret and anger. You can also feel more content and accepting of what is now in both your personal and work life, though you can still strive to make changes to make things even better.

These feelings of gratitude can also support any religious faith you have, and they can bring more abundance into your life. In part, this happens because you attract into your life what you put out, so having this positive, welcoming, giving outlook brings many future benefits.

Then, too, this attitude of gratitude can draw others to you, since you are more positive, giving, and humble, which can contribute to better relationships along with having a fuller, more abundant, more satisfying life.

By contrast, people who are not grateful can turn others off with their negative, complaining attitude, so they tend not to be as successful.

In short, as discussed in the introduction to each section and expressed in the quotes, there are many benefits to feeling gratitude and sharing your grateful feelings with others.

Here are some things you can do to feel and express more gratitude in your life:

1) Keep a gratitude journal or add a section to your journal where you write down what you are most grateful for that day.

2) Make a list of the 10 to 20 things you are most grateful for in your life.

3) Write up your favorite quotes about gratitude in large print on separate sheets of paper. Then, post the quotes around your house where you can see them each day.

4) Take a gratitude walk around your neighborhood or nearby park. Think about how you are grateful for the beauty you see around you as you walk.

5) Pair up with a friend or business associate and take about 5-10 minutes to share what you are grateful for that day or that past week. Or form a weekly or monthly gratitude group of 3-10 people, where you share with one another for about 30 minutes to an hour about your experiences of gratitude for that week or month.

6) Create a Vision Board or Vision Board Book, in which you gather images of the things you are most grateful for and paste them on your board or in your book. Then, post the board or carry the book with you, so you can look at these images from time to time to remind you to feel gratitude for all of these great things in your life.

7) Create a list of 5-10 people you feel grateful towards and think about what they did. If you haven't thanked them for a while or at all, call them or thank them in person if you will be seeing them soon.

8) Do a gratitude meditation for about 10-15 minutes on your own or with others. During this time, get relaxed, close your eyes, and while you are in this calm, meditative state, visualize what you feel grateful for and feel the glow of gratitude flow through your body. If you want to thank someone, see yourself doing this, experience their satisfaction and happiness as you thank them, and feel good yourself.

9) If you experience a difficult situation or person, stay calm, remind yourself to make the best of the situation, think of it as an experience to learn and grow from, and as you can, do something you like to do. Also, think about how you have overcome other problems in the past, so you see yourself gaining confidence and power to deal with whatever problem you are confronting now. Reminding yourself of your past success in dealing with problems can help you put aside feelings of anger, sadness, jealousy, wanting revenge, or whatever negativity you are experiencing, while you replace these with gratitude and other positive feelings.

10) Think of ways you can show your gratitude towards those around you so you can strengthen those relationships. For example, you might praise someone's work to them or at a group meeting. You might leave a note on someone's desk at work or send a card to friend to say thanks for something. Or you might give someone an appropriate gift to say thank you for a referral that led to a new personal relationship or increased business.

11) And now over to you. Think of other ways you might experience gratitude or share your feelings of thankfulness with others.

ABOUT THE AUTHOR

GINI GRAHAM SCOTT, Ph.D., J.D., is a nationally known writer, consultant, speaker, and seminar leader, specializing in business and work relationships, professional and personal development, social trends, science, and crime. She has published over 50 books with major publishers. She has worked with dozens of clients on books and proposals on popular business, self-help, and memoirs. Additionally, she writes film scripts and has produced 10 feature films, documentaries, and TV series. She writes the copy and works with a team of associates who help clients with social media posts, publicity, promotional videos, and web design.

She is the founder of Changemakers Publishing, featuring books on business, psychology, self-help, and social trends. The company has published over 200 print and e-books and over 150 audiobooks. She has licensed several dozen books for foreign sales, including the UK, Russia, Korea, Spain, and Japan.

She has received national media exposure for her books, including appearances on *Good Morning America, Oprah,* and *CNN*.

Her books on business include:
Work With Me (Davies-Black Publishing)
A Survival Guide for Working with Humans (AMACOM)
Lies and Liars: How and Why Sociopaths Lie (Skyhorse Publishing)
Her books on self-help, health, and wellness include:
Mind Power: Picture Your Way to Success (Simon & Schuster)
The Empowered Mind: (Simon & Schuster)
Want It, See It, Get It: Visualize Your Way to Success (AMACOM)

Her films which are in distribution include *Driver* (Gravitas Ventures), Infidelity (Green Apple), *The New Age of Aging* (Factory Films) and *Me, My Dog and I* and *Rescue Me* (Random Media). The films are showcased at www.changemakersproductionsfilms.com.

Scott is active in a number of community and business groups, including the Lafayette, Pleasant Hill, and Walnut Creek Chambers of Commerce. She does workshops and seminars on the topics of her books and on self-publishing.

She received her PhD in Sociology from the University of California, Berkeley, her JD from the University of San Francisco Law School, and five MAs at Cal State University, East Bay, including in Anthropology, Mass Communications and Organizational/Consumer/Audience Behavior, Popular Culture and Lifestyles, and Communication.

OTHER BOOKS BY THE AUTHOR

Mind Power: Picture Your Way to Success

The Empowered Mind: How to Harness the Creative Force Within You

More Success and Happiness

Affirming Your Success

Turn Your Dreams into Reality

The Vision Board Book

100 Ways to Gain More Success

What's Your Personality Type

CHANGEMAKERS PUBLISHING
3527 Mt. Diablo Blvd., #273
Lafayette, CA 94549
www.changemakerspublishing.com
(925) 385-0608 . changemakers@pacbell.net